Come to Think About It

Associations…

by
Frank Olsson

Order this book online at www.trafford.com
or email orders@trafford.com

Most Trafford titles are also available at major online book retailers.

Note for Librarians: A cataloguing record for this book is available from Library
and Archives Canada at www.collectionscanada.ca/amicus/index-e.html

Printed in Victoria, BC, Canada.

ISBN: 978-1-4269-1457-7 (sc)

*Our mission is to efficiently provide the world's finest, most comprehensive book publishing
service, enabling every author to experience success. To find out how to publish your book, your
way, and have it available worldwide, visit us online at www.trafford.com*

Trafford rev. 8/11/09

 www.trafford.com

North America & international
toll-free: 1 888 232 4444 (USA & Canada)
phone: 250 383 6864 ♦ fax: 812 355 4082

*Association...mental connection between related ideas; an idea, recollection or feeling mental connected with another. / Oxford Dictionary

Contents

Introduction

To the peoples, nations and men of every language, who live in the world: may you prosper greatly! Daniel 4: 1

Ever since my school days, people and human nature captured my interest more than the sciences. I liked those too, but only insofar as I could see that what was at hand had some kind of human angle and meaning. I had a happy childhood in a middle class suburb of Stockholm, Sweden, where most suburbs and people are middle class. My lucky break was a year as an exchange student at a Michigan High School. I did the mandatory Swedish military service and became a Captain in the engineering troops; then studied law and economics. My first job was with the City of Stockholm and later I transferred to banking. Having an international outlook, I decided to take up an offer of an overseas assignment with the World Bank in Africa. From there my career took me to Singapore, London, Wellington, Auckland, Singapore again and then Tokyo, before returning to Auckland. Each year I return to Sweden to enjoy the lovely Nordic summers with family and friends.

During my career I have come across many different cultures and challenges. I found myself in the position where I've been asked to guide and motivate people from varied backgrounds. This led me to consider what makes people act the way they do and what it takes to increase happiness, and perhaps productivity, and success at the same time. Some of my thoughts are expressed in this book.

My wife's Linda, fiftieth birthday party was arranged in Petra, Jordan. On the way there we spent a week in Jerusalem, met up with friends and hired a bus to take us all to Petra. Knowing some time in advance that we were going to Jerusalem, and being a keen reader, I decided to read the Bible to give some background to what we would be seeing in the area.

During the reading I marked out passages that I found profound, positive and with some general relevance to my contemporaries and me. This process gave me just less than one page from each of the sixty-six books of the Bible. I have not attempted to make a full and fair summary of the Bible but only to highlight what I found particularly important.

In a few places in the Bible it is suggested that women are not man's equal and I have not recorded anything about this as I feel time has rendered such thoughts obsolete. Also slavery seems to have been an accepted order by Biblical authors, but I have not picked it up as over the millennia our views also on this matter have changed. Similarly the views expressed in a few places on homosexuality have changed in modern times to reflect love and tolerance. The key message about love does in my view render all the three biases referred to obsolete. My extracts represent no more than perhaps one percent of the Bible.

Once I had collated my notes of the various books, I thought I should develop the concept a bit further. Reading a book like the Bible inevitably makes you reflect on everything you have experienced and thought. I wanted to note down some of these thoughts, and decided to do it as a short note to each of the Biblical books.

Over lunch with a friend in London, I discussed the concept of putting a few ideas to paper under the structure of sixty-six notes to the books of the Bible. Calling it 'Associations (i.e. this is what I think right now having read this biblical book or summary of the book) would allow me to write absolutely anything that came to mind. No problem with sticking to the subject or countering digressions - just invite and accept them and treat them as realities of life. How readable is that going to be? That is for you to determine! It provided me an easy approach to follow and pursue. My friend thought it a good idea and that was all the encouragement I needed.

The method of composing sixty-six brief notes allowed me to express some views within my limited concentration span. So I started the journey in Singapore in July 2000 and less than two years later finished the odyssey in Tokyo, to which City we relocated in 2001. During this time, I traveled to New Zealand, Australia, India, Indonesia, Hong Kong, Thailand and Malaysia, as well as through Europe by rail. In

2003 we all moved back to New Zealand and I have been editing my initial writing off and on.

My belief is that we should try to integrate things that stir us and move our innermost beings more with our everyday lives, making ethics and love integral parts of daily conduct including the way we do business. A stronger commitment to ethics is not a necessary evil, or a price we have to pay, it really is adorning life with beauty and meaning, without which everything is barren and futile. Instinctively, many people believe there must be a better, more human, more inclusive and more positive way.

In my role as a manager of staff and in serving customers, I have always tried to create a dance of souls by some relevant reference to ethics, beauty and love. Sometimes I felt the dance was on; sometimes I felt I was dancing alone. But generally the effort has been well received and I have found the yearning for adding meaning to monetary measures and incentives very strong, as is the potential to unlock dormant energy and enthusiasm.

My hope is that anyone who opens this book will find at least something of interest within it. It gives me great pleasure to be your guide for this excursion.

Frank Olsson
Auckland, November 2003

1. Genesis

As long as the earth endures,
Seedtime and harvest
cold and heat,
summer and winter,
day and night,
will never cease." 8: 21- 22

Never again will all life be cut off by the waters of a flood; never again will there be a flood to destroy the earth. 9: 11

They said to each other, "Come let's make brick instead of stone, and bitumen for mortar." Then they said, "Come let us build ourselves a city, with a tower that reaches to the heavens, so that we may make a name for ourselves and not be scattered over the face of the whole earth." The LORD said, "If as one people speaking the same language they have begun to do this, then nothing they plan to do will be impossible for them." 11: 3 - 6

Abimelech said to Isaac, "Move away from us; you have become too powerful for us." 26: 16

When Isaac caught the smell of Jacob's cloths, he blessed him and said,

"Ah the smell of my son
is like the smell of a field
that the LORD has blessed.
May God give you of heaven's dew
and of earth's richness -
an abundance of grain and new wine.

May nations serve you and peoples bow down to you.
Be lord over your brothers,
and may the sons of your mother bow down to you.
May those who curse you be cursed
and those who bless you be blessed" 27: 27 - 29

Jacob served seven years to get Rachel, but they seemed like only a few days to him because of his love for her. 29: 20

The warder paid no attention to anything under Joseph's care, because the LORD was with Joseph and gave him success in whatever he did. 39: 23

Joseph said to his brothers, "Don't be afraid. Am I in the place of God? You intended to harm me, but God intended it for good to accomplish what is now being done, the saving of many lives. I will provide for you and your children." And he reassured them and spoke kindly to them. 50: 20 – 22

Associations...

1. Genesis

People united and speaking the same language can again and again achieve that which may have looked impossible. In the last century the English language, and more recently the Internet, have enabled a vast proportion of the world's peoples to communicate with each other. And although it helps to speak the same language, it is perhaps not necessary for communication and understanding. If values and goals can be generally accepted, then the basis for our communication is already the same. This international language is one of love and compassion. I have worked with people in Europe, Africa, America and Asia and personally experienced that showing interest in and concern for the next person, whether up or down 'the ladder' almost always results in empathy and compassion. Whoever truly has my interest at heart I am keen to work with and assist in achieving extraordinary results! An environment of faith, trust, and the absence of fear, creates the good soil for energy, creativity and ingenuity. This appeals to the spirit which is necessary for reaching the highest levels of achievement.

Organizations and countries perform below potential when there is poor alignment of the will of the people and the task at hand. I believe a majority of people innately want to do well for themselves and to others. We want to help the group get results and be personally appreciated as a important link in overall achievement. To be worthy of being a leader is to have some understanding of motivation, and to be able to touch the spirit and speak to the soul. Behavior of this sort is understood and appreciated across any language, race, religion or other real or perceived barrier. Schools and organizations must focus more on building character as the highest skills without the character to position those skills may be a curse and no blessing. Lack of skills may slow perceived progress a little but only when good character and values are at hand can we be on the right track and moving at higher speed on the wrong track can spell disaster.

Anyone with much power needs to be careful in drawing on and demonstrating the power. The very nature of exercising power is to make people act not to their will but the will of the authority. Only if we voluntarily accept the merit of such authority will we act with energy and enthusiasm. If we don't find the required behavior sensible we will inevitably do a half-hearted job. Being made to do what I don't want to do may breed resentment. I am not talking here about the little things we perhaps reluctantly need to accept doing for the benefit of a functioning family or community but of major things that the powerful can coerce the governed to do.

Working together gives a great sense of purpose and achievement. Together we can do things we cannot even contemplate on our own. Power and potential are great when we are driven by our free will. Add force, and the energy sooner or later dissipates. Taking undue advantage of the other's contribution discourages application and contribution. Only when we are convinced of the merits of our toil will we produce the best results. Motivation once fully turned on is unstoppable.

The only justification for making any decision on behalf of others is that they have volunteered to vest their confidence in you, a delegation that can only be earned through respect and which can at any time be recalled. Any other representation is exploitation and oppression. In a democracy we must protect not only any minority. We must protect the smallest minority of all, the individual.

It is obvious to me that large groups of the world population now feel that USA and its incumbent president (George W. Bush as I write this) are too powerful. The world will only reluctantly accept such power if it is curtailed by checks and input from others and exercised with love, humility and wisdom. The founding fathers of the US constitution spent much time trying to limit power. They would most likely turn over in their graves if they saw how their creation had slipped away. Deterioration of good concepts and intentions are often gradual such that no one can really see what is happening until many years later we have created something highly undesirable.

We must stop and consider that growth is only useful if it is good growth that factors in the wellbeing of people and nature. Our schools and education systems should try to bring more of a holistic understanding to students and rate those student highest who combine skills with good character. Measuring may of course be challenging but to disregard what is important because it is difficult to measure can only be likened to 'head-in-the-sand' stupidity. And bad behavior, whether corporate or other, must be neither encouraged nor tolerated. Government should not be anti-business. But both business and government must be anti bad business practices. Business activity needs to align and not be contrary to the good life we all aspire to.

Teaching based on diagrams with x and y axis suggests that the world is flat. Many things are easier to comprehend if we make such assumptions. But if the third dimension not represented in the diagram is the crucial driver of behavior and events, our teaching falls flat too. To understand, respect and capture the spirit and imagination of people is crucial for good results and thus has to be learned and acquired in parallel to traditional skills.

The three last passages I have included above from 'Genesis' all speak of love. Love is at the core of who we are and what we do and the key component in parenting, managing and leading. The Russian author Leo Tolstoy says in his book 'Resurrection:' "There are no circumstances when one may deal with human beings without love." Love is the ultimate counterbalance to all conceivable ills and evils that may befall mankind. 'He reassured them and spoke kindly to them.'

2. Exodus

The Ten Commandments:
You shall have no other Gods before me.
You shall not make for yourself and idol,
You shall not misuse the name of the Lord
Remember the Sabbath day on which you shall not do any work, nor anyone else.
Honor your father and your mother so that you may live long in the land,
You shall not murder,
You shall not commit adultery,
You shall not steal,
You shall not bear false testimony against your neighbor,
You shall not covet your neighbor's house, his wife, servant, ox or donkey or anything that belongs to your neighbor. 20: 8 - 17

Do not ill treat an alien or oppress him, for you were aliens in Egypt. 22: 21

If you lend money to one of my people among you who is needy, do not be like a moneylender. Charge him no interest. If you take your neighbor's cloak as a pledge, return it to him by sunset, because his cloak is the only covering he has for his body. What else will he sleep in? When he cries out to me, I will hear for I am compassionate. 22: 25 - 28

Do not spread false reports. Do not help the wicked man by being a malicious witness. Do not follow the crowd in doing wrong. When you give testimony in a lawsuit, do not pervert justice by siding with the crowd, and do not show favoritism to a poor man in his lawsuit. 23:1-4

Have nothing to do with a false charge and do not put an innocent or honest person to death, for I will not acquit the guilty. 23: 6

Do not accept a bribe, for a bribe binds those who see and twist the words of the righteous. 23: 9

For six years you are to sow the fields and harvest the crops, but the seventh year, let the land lie un-ploughed and unused. Then the poor among your people may get food from it, and the wild animals may eat what they leave. Do the same with your vineyard and your olive grove. 23: 10 - 12

It is not the sound of victory,
it is not the sound of defeat,
it is the sound of singing that I hear 32: 18

Associations...

2 Exodus

We do need some rules in order to limit fear and provide a basis for love and compassion. The most obvious ones speak up against murder and theft, which if not contained, erode quality of life and prevent progress. And we need to be driven by benevolence and not fall prey to mysticism or magic. We need to act considerately and caringly under the realization that our actions determine or impact how we ourselves will be treated. These rules are more or less interdependent. If one or two are violated it can easily erode respect for the whole package. However, judgment will always enter into the picture, as there are situations under which all these rules may have to be broken. Key here is to be pure in motive and driven by love and compassion, as inclusive and widely defined as possible.

The line on treating aliens well is often repeated in the Bible. Virtually all the peoples in the world have been immigrants at some stage in history. As an immigrant you may be quite vulnerable with lack of property and friends. It is very easy for the people already established to take advantage of their position to try to reject and discriminate against immigrants, wanting to protect the status quo or prevent any dilution of their privileged position. Enlightened people will see that this is not the way to go, as it is inconsistent with inclusive love and the win-win philosophy (the Golden Rule). Again good judgment comes in, as there are many calls that need to be made even in relation to the flow of immigrants. Key here is 'good character' in the people and their leaders such that motives for decisions and actions are made transparent and driven by broader interest than that of self or a small or large group. The just interest of <u>all</u> must be considered.

Banking is a very fundamental Industry in a sophisticated interconnected world like the one we live in. Having worked with and for banks for twenty-five years, I have seen both visionaries and bigots in the industry. The two perhaps most common banking services are deposits and mortgage loans, safe keeping excess funds paying some level of interest and putting people in homes. These basic services and similar services for corporations serve good and legitimate purposes and participating banks are generally kept in check by regulation and competition.

However, the unrestrained marketing of consumer credit that encourages people to spend money they don't have for purposes they cannot afford to drive the banks' profit and volume, is more circumspect. But surely business is about profits and shareholder return? Is it? If the financial results are achieved in 'immoral' ways, there is a growing risk of a reaction and the building of bad will and erosion of brand value. Transactions need to be assessed not only as to whether they are within the law, but also if they are serving anything other than narrow self interest. Otherwise company good will is eroded.

And people of good character do not want to work for unscrupulous organizations. This means that such organizations become a home for people weak on values - potential cancer cells in our society. Good corporate governance must set and check the standards. If society at large is a looser, but I come out a winner, how sustainable is that?

With working experience in Africa and Asia on the one hand and Sweden, the UK and New Zealand on the other, I have seen up close both essentially corrupt and essentially non-corrupt societies. There can be no doubt about the devastating effect of corruption and graft. What these things mean is that people in responsible positions compromise duty for personal wealth in a most corrosive way.

The role model effect of leadership cannot be underestimated and when subordinates see their seniors being driven not by the weal of their organization or their government or the people, but by enriching themselves, then all others tend to follow suite. This reduces energy, commitment and compassion and fuels greed, egoism and impropriety, all things that impede progress and quality of life.

Nine months into my World Bank contract in Nairobi I resigned to take up another job in Singapore. I thought the job I was set to do in Africa needed doing, and I found that my skills set and experience were a nearly perfect match for the job required. But when every proposal and idea fell on deaf ears for lack of personal gain by the recipient decision makers, I realized the screaming need for change of leadership practices for any achievement at all to be possible. This was out of my reach and not on the agenda. My choice then was to opt out, or stay and just enjoy my tax-free salary and excellent personal living conditions. Of course I did the former, but have continued to think about how to tackle corruption and argue against it whenever I have a chance.

Just like agricultural land, humans need to relax as well. If you constantly exert pressure for more return there is a real risk of ultimately exhausting the resource completely. People need brakes every hour, every day, every week if they are to be wholesome and retain ingenuity. They say that in Japan, one problem with graduates is that once students finish school they have been exposed to so much memorizing / learning pressure that they have suppressed the independent thought process so necessary for innovation. Often the sense of life and worth also get dented with stress, which, sometimes even causes suicide. The parallels to land and agriculture are striking. Land and people need rest and time for crop rotation and alternative uses. People need to nurture their souls and not just be better and better robots. And sharing a little of the fruits of your labor is an investment for the future.

Song and music - just spending quality time together - is perhaps the ultimate purpose of human existence. It is up to all of us to ensure that these things don't only get residual time slots, but that they are given prime time in our lives. The artist is not doing a less important work than the welder, in fact one needs the other. Art can virtually never be done for selfish purposes - its very nature is that it is done for others. More room for art will make for a better society!

3. Leviticus

I f anyone deceives his neighbor about something entrusted or left in his care or stolen, he must make restitution in full and add a fifth of the value to it and give it all to the owner. 6: 5

Do not go over your vineyard a second time or pick up the grapes that have fallen. Leave them for the poor and the alien. 19: 10
Do not hold back the wages of a hired man overnight 19: 13
Do not hate your brother in your heart. Rebuke your neighbor frankly so that you will not share in his guilt. 19: 17
Do not seek revenge or bear a grudge against one of your people, but love your neighbor as yourself. 19: 18

Rise in the presence of the aged, show respect for the elderly. 19:32
When an alien lives with you in your land, do not ill-treat him. The alien living with you must be treated as one of your native born. Love him as yourself, for you were aliens in Egypt. 19: 33
On the first day of the seventh month you are to have a day of rest, a sacred assembly commemorated with trumpet blasts. 23: 23
If one of your countrymen becomes poor and is unable to support himself among you, help him as you would an alien or a temporary resident, so that he can continue to live among you. You must not lend him money at interest or sell him food for a profit. 25: 35 - 37
Set the value of a male between the ages of twenty and sixty at fifty shekels of silver, and if it is a female, set her value at thirty shekels. 27:3 – 4

Associations.

3 Leviticus

If we don't deliver on trust put in us, this comes at a high cost and in fact nothing much would work in this world, if in the majority of cases we couldn't expect people to do what they have committed to do. Anyone who tries to take undue advantage of trust must be brought back in line. And he must be set back far enough for him to experience, and for all others to see, that such course of action is unprofitable. Particularly in this day and age, with almost perfect information and communication, it is difficult to gain sustainable advantage at someone else's expense. The world is slowly improving in this respect and in places where graft and corruption are rife, it is clear that economic progress and investment are suffering.

Empathy and care for the less fortunate is part and parcel of humanity. Where would the world be without it? Where would you be without it? Leave something on the table for the other person. Generosity builds good will and friendships and acts as insurance for any and all, should misfortune strike. Every fifth person cannot keep up for a shorter or longer period. Help him/her. But when societies are thus arranged that most people need assistance regularly for survival, there may well be something seriously out of balance.

Pay your debts quickly. Don't hold back because you can. What you are entitled to do and what is in your long-term interest may well be very different. This is particularly true if you hold the position of strength. The biggest single asset in most present-day companies is goodwill and bad practices deplete goodwill. Even values not represented in your books need to be nurtured and looked after. Don't get too smart for your own good. To take advantage of someone else's misfortune or position of weakness is a sure way of resentment and value depletion.

Don't stop at yourself, don't stop at your family, don't stop at your hometown, don't stop at your race, don't stop at your country - let your interests, compassion and love be all-inclusive. There is no us and them, only us - we are in it together. This attitude is so obviously beneficial when you think about it because it eliminates negative energy and it increases opportunity. Less downside, more upside - no right thinking person would reject a formula like that. Fear and destruction depletes value for all. Fair and equitable treatment is not enough, we must add to that care and affection. Love!

Rest is not the enemy of work, it is a prerequisite. Work is a tool for a better life, not the other way around. Most production is in fact geared towards helping people create a better more livable life, improving the quality of rest and recreation. If work makes people miserable, this will inevitably cause resentment, reducing viability and prospects for market success. Workers, customers and investors will ultimately notice bad practices lack of corps d'esprit and do business elsewhere.

The only reasonable attitude to immigration and immigrants is tolerance and compassion. In each developed country there is a minority who are against immigration. Mixing people, races and cultures holds out hope for more trade, and better understanding and co-operation. Countries that have welcomed immigration have generally fared better than those who haven't. Aspects of love are tolerance and open-mindedness. All religion as far as I have been able to ascertain, require love to be extended to both friend and foreigner.

Part of open mindedness is diversity including gender diversity. I have noted above one of the few passages in the bible that value women less than men. I have to believe that this is cultural and historic, possibly relating to physical strength. I have no doubt that in the era of the knowledge economy, women are in no way man's inferior and the complementarities of the genders strongly advocate the merits of diversity.

We all know that Asians particularly honor their elders. Sooner or later we will all be of that category. Most people work very hard for many years to try to get their off spring better conditions than they themselves were able to enjoy. To reward such unselfish behavior when the older generation ultimately needs assistance for survival makes a lot of human sense.

4. Numbers

Assign to each man the things he is to carry. 4: 32

M oses was a very humble man, more humble than anyone else on the face of the earth. 12: 3

The LORD is slow to anger, abounding in love, and forgiving sin and rebellion. 14: 18

The same laws and regulations will apply both to you and to the alien living among you. 15: 16

Each inheritance is to be distributed by lot among the larger and smaller groups. 26: 56

If a man dies and leaves no son, give his inheritance over to his daughter. If he has no daughter, give his inheritance to his brothers. If he has no brothers, give his inheritance to his father's brothers. If his father had no brothers, give his inheritance to the nearest relative in his clan, that he may possess it. 26: 8 - 12

Do not pollute the land where you are. 35: 3

Associations...

4 Numbers

A beautiful autumn day, this thirteenth day of October 2001 in Shibuya-ku, a suburb of Tokyo. I was a bit tired this morning after a hard week but with a short run in the morning sun followed by a shower I feel a lot better. I read a few chapters in my book on love and sex as viewed by different religions. Went for a walk to get some bottled water and fetch the dry cleaning. Received four nice high stools, bought two weeks earlier in Asakusa, for our kitchen bar counter. Linda was a bit worried we might not get them as I had lost my receipt, but I was very confident that quid pro quo would eventuate.

Bringing the dog, I went to the little bakery in twenty-five degrees sunshine to get some brown bread for lunch. Made nice sandwiches with ham, onion and tomato for the three of us, which we had together with some eggs and coffee with milk, sitting at the bar counter on our new chairs. Pretty ordinary! Pretty nice! Television keeps reporting twenty-four hours a day on the bombings and refugees in Afghanistan. Does it make any sense or is it complete madness? Quite disturbing either way!

Back to my associations! A vast majority of people want to make a contribution, want to help out, and want to feel needed and meaningful. That is part of confidence and self-respect. We must try to allow all to share in this sense of inclusion and belonging by providing training and education and invite all into the community of work and effort. This is where a lot of foreign aid goes wrong in that it offers a sharing in surplus outputs but donor countries are quite hostile to shared inputs. Africans and others need to be able to produce and sell to survive and grow, and not only be on the receiving end, excluded from trade by punitive tariffs. This is a welfare trap! When I worked in Africa I got the impression that if all aid was cancelled tomorrow in exchange for free trade of agricultural and other basic produce, Africa would be much better off. But, no, we don't want to do anything that threatens our jobs? The best thing we can export is jobs, i.e. the ability of the recipients to gradually look after themselves. This is required for true constructive aid and sharing. Anything short of this is a waste of time. As world welfare is not a zero sum game helping your neighbor is more of an investment than a cost.

Humility, compassion and integrity are key components of leadership and civilized conduct. On humility I had an interesting experience at New York offices of Goldman Sachs, the investment bank, in the early eighties. As important customers of the bank, my senior colleague and I were ushered into the managing partner's (John Weinberg) office and, as we had a brief chat around his coffee table, my colleague asked: "Why do you keep such a huge wastebasket next to your desk?" This was a dustbin-sized receptacle that looked a bit out of place. His quick answer was: "When I feel too great sometimes, I go and sit in it for a while." Even if this was a bit novel, we laughed at his witticism. It doesn't hurt to consider daily that we were born naked and we will once go that way too. Too many people take themselves far too seriously. Waratte ii tomo! (It is ok to laugh).

'Slow to anger, abounding in love, and quick to forgive.' If we could get our children to understand and embrace the concepts covered in these ten words we would have a basis and framework on which to build sound and lasting progress. All other skills may be worth nothing unless set against a background of benevolence and love. And yet we don't even have ethics as a subject in our schools, and in our businesses it normally attracts only marginal interest compared to professional skills. In our pursuit of Utopia, this has to change.

In the last two hundred years so many human problems have been addressed and solved. To get to the next level we have to focus on compassion and love, and an all inclusive win-win formula. This has everything to do with business and government and education. If you don't know where you are going, there is nothing to test progress against. Corporations get more and more serious about understanding and managing risk to protect shareholder value. The greatest risks by far are weak values and lack of character - forgetting the greater purpose of what we are doing.

Of the remaining lines I picked the one on aliens, as we need to understand that we are all the same people regardless of color, gender, religion, origination etc. This message is more important than ever and in many ways should be easier to convey due to the incredible increase in travel, and the use of Television and Internet. The bible (and other scriptures as well) suggests that when we have a windfall gain, we should consider those less fortunate as well. This makes sense. Perhaps the greatest sensation most of us have in life is the awesome beauty of nature which gives us food for body and soul. One of our most important obligations is to align all our actions that this wonder and source of all good is not impinged on but preserved unencumbered to the end of time. Amen.

5. Deuteronomy

Keep all his decrees and commands that I give you, so that you may enjoy long life. Be careful to obey so that it may go well with you and that you may increase greatly in a land flowing with milk and honey, just as the Lord, the God of your fathers, promised you. 6: 2-4

He humbled you, causing you to hunger and then feeding you with manna, which neither you nor your fathers had known, to teach you that man does not live on bread alone but on every word that comes from the mouth of the LORD.

The LORD, your God is bringing you into a good land - a land with streams and pools of water, with springs flowing in the valleys and hills; a land with wheat and barley, vines and fig trees, pomegranates, olive oil and honey; a land where bread will not be scarce and you will lack nothing; a land where the rocks are iron and you can dig copper out of the hills. 8: 3 - 10

Fix these words of mine in your hearts and minds; tie them as symbols on your hands and bind them on your foreheads. Teach them to your children, talking about them when you sit at home and when you walk the road, when you lie down and when you get up. Write them on the doorframes of your houses and your gates, so that your days and the days of your children may be many..11: 18 - 20

Do not be hard-hearted or tight-fisted towards your brother. Rather be open-handed and freely lend him whatever he needs. Give generously to him and do so without a grudging heart and God will bless you in all your work and everything you put your hand to. 15:8-13

Do not pervert justice or show partiality. Do not accept a bribe, for a bribe blinds the eyes of the wise and twists the words of the righteous.

Follow justice and justice alone so that you may possess the land you have been given. 16: 19 - 20

Follow carefully this law and these decrees and don't consider yourself better than your brothers and don't turn from the law to the right or to the left. 17: 19 - 20

Whatever your lips utter you must be sure to do, because you made your vow freely with your own mouth. 23: 23

When you are harvesting in your field and you overlook a sheaf, do not go back and get it. Leave it for the alien, the fatherless and the widow. 24: 19

Carefully follow the terms of this covenant, so that you may prosper in everything you do. 29: 9

Now choose life, so that you and your children may live. 30: 20

Associations...

5 Deuteronomy

Life has to be guided by certain values. Although these differ somewhat around the world it is clear that there is strong resemblance and commonality. The measure of the quality of the values is to what extent they are commensurate with, and promote, happiness. All Ten Commandments in fact make a lot of sense in this respect. Knowing that all of us cannot stay on the road all of the time, there must be provision for inviting digressers back on the road, delicately designed such that the cure in itself doesn't produce undue fear or undermine happiness. That cure is forgiveness and love. It may not be perfect in all situations, but like democracy, it beats all available alternatives. Always!

Our TV channel 15 spends Twenty-four hours a day talking about money. Quite sickening really! Man cannot live on bread alone. So much beauty, so much to see, so much to do, so much opportunity! And a culture that teaches you to focus all your energy to hoard up - for a house, for a car, for health, for children, for old age. If we lose sight of the valley and the hills, the olive oil and the honey, what use is all the rest? There is no goal, there is no then, and there is no end. There is only now and love. For you and your children and grandchildren and all mankind! If you love what you do you are blessed, if not, be sure to add some spice or olive oil.

You are what you think. Read, think and talk about good things, good values, optimism and generosity, forgiveness and love. Like music! This will help you to stay on course when you face life, when you have to act quickly, when there is little time to think. Talk to your children and your friends, and try to be a role model. Role modeling means being demanding on self rather than on others. Morality is about improving yourself. Generosity, reciprocity, generosity! With simple means we can build a better world.

Giving is living. Seneca said: 'I shall consider myself owning nothing but what I have given away with dignity.' Giving creates credits. In a bank, all the money the bank has given out is called 'assets' and all the money that is has received is called 'liabilities.' Even if banks are not necessarily what first comes to mind when you think about generosity, this may all the same be an interesting analogy.

One of the disadvantages with socialism is that the state monopolizes giving and generosity by taking an inordinate amount of money off people. Those in government seem to think: 'We know better how to use the money, and will give most of it back anyway, particularly to our supporters, after deducting enough for ourselves that we can have a good lifestyle.' You cannot replace the need for virtuous individuals by leaving it all to government and bureaucracy. Collectives have no soul. No soul, no life. Finally, we must remember that part of generosity is receiving graciously as well. Allowing others to give! It is a two way street.

When you feel something is not right you must have the guts to speak up. It can always be done constructively and lovingly. Like: Wouldn't it perhaps be better if...? Not speaking up, not trying to promote good values for fear of reprisal can be a mild form of graft and bribery. In serious cases you extinguish yourself and become robot-like, losing key aspects of your humanity. When power is flaunted it invites fear, suppresses participation and initiative and takes value out.

Deliver on your commitments. Trust is the lubrication of friendships, business and trade. Running business and trade without trust is like running an engine without oil. It soon grinds to a halt.

The biggest motivator is undoubtedly 'a great cause.' This is probably the most underutilized motivator in big business. Possibly because top management doesn't understand it or is perhaps stumbling on power, greed, ignorance and incompetence, and is preoccupied with short term external pressures. The cure is vision, generosity and love. And incidentally, none of these can be expressed numerically. Numbers are either historic or useless. Numbers are not visionary. 'Now choose life, so that you and your children may live.' Deuteronomy 30: 20

II. Joshua through Chronicles with Associations

6. Joshua

Joshua is essentially about the Israelites moving east across the Jordan "conquering cities - including Jericho - wiping out everything breathing and setting the cities on fire". Quite cruel and grim narrative! If there is anything positive to take out of it, it would be that a united group of high spirited people fighting for a common cause can be very successful.

Be strong and courageous. Do not be terrified; do not be discouraged. 1: 9
Not one of their enemies withstood them. 21: 44

Associations...

6 Joshua

In the far distance I see five sun lit skyscrapers against a background of a clear blue October sky. Nearer there are some white and red brick residential low rises. And closer yet are the hanging electrical wires, appreciated by none but the crows and perhaps the dogs, for whom they provide useful poles with regular intervals. Just outside my window there are a number of trees. The window has an outer net part to keep the bugs out, then the glass and finally two beautiful sliding screens, shoji. Blue, silvery grey, red, white, green and finally the white and brown of the screens, providing a lovely inviting and inspiring vista for trying to gather some thoughts on a Saturday morning. It is indeed nice with a little writing space of one's own next to a window to the world.

A cool breeze comes through the slightly open window. Not many sounds, other than a few little birds and some big loud-mouthed crows besides the odd vehicle slowly moving by. The narrowness of the streets forces drivers to be gentle and cautious. It is going to be another shining day with very comfortable afternoon temperatures. Tokyo, on the same parallel as northern Africa or southern Spain, enjoys a near perfect climate and yet four distinct seasons. Having lived on the equator in Africa and Asia, we quite appreciate the seasons; the warm season, the cooling, the cold, the thawing, the rebirth and the therapeutic flow of warmth again. And all this without the deadly grip of winter, which I sometimes experienced growing up near the North Pole.

A sense of visual depth is important for the soul and for your dreams. My good friend in Melbourne who just bought a nice apartment in Oriental Bay in Wellington, New Zealand, said that his father lived out his life without a view and my friend really wanted to secure a view for himself and his wife. A view helps stimulate broadmindedness and farsightedness. All should be blessed with a view of fields, mountains, the sea or a river. And views represent intangible value that has been made tangible in house prices. In Auckland, the City of sails, any house that commands a view of the perfectly symmetrical volcano island of Rangitoto fetches at least one hundred thousand dollars more than a house not so fortunate. And in many other locations, absolute sea front often doubles the price compared to one notch further in. The difference? The view! The unhindered space for the soul!

My good friend from Cullen in Scotland took me for a balloon ride on my birthday, December twenty fourth, five years ago. Looking at the little basket on the ground and the six people to fit into it, it looked almost undoable. But once in the air, commanding a three hundred and sixty degree view of the world from an elevated quiet vantage point, the sense of crowdedness completely disappeared. Sweeping along the treetops looking at cows and sheep and little farms and lakes with the blue Pacific visible in the distance provided infinite space for the soul. The health and the spirit of the soul will carry the body any day. Cooking with gas! A truly delightful experience!

As to the second to last sentence for those who don't know, it is an English expression used to describe things going really well. My good friend Richard, with a lovely house on the Coromandel Peninsula East of Auckland, uses the expression all the time. He draws on gas, the clean and easy to use fuel, in converting raw material into delicious meals. The cooking and eating takes place on the veranda, facing the sea with waves rolling in unhindered from the Americas across the world's biggest ocean. And with a glass of chilled white New Zealand wine for the cook and his adviser - what better expression can there be than 'Cooking with gas!'

Getting on a bit now and we have decided to go to Yokohama for the day to get some new impressions and test the train system. We start with half an hour's walk to Shibuya station, ask for directions, pay the Yen 260 for the trip, and we are away on a mini adventure. After another half hour we arrive in Yokohama and are faced with one of these huge Japanese stations with exits left, right and centre. We manage to get out on the East side, which turns out to be the right side, and find an information booth. The kind lady behind the counter provides us with a map and I ask for a furniture shop and she circles a big area and draws a line on the map for how to get there. Kantan desu! (Easy).

We start moving as directed over a little river and on to a newly developed area with a big car free street in the middle and a huge conference centre at the end facing the sea. All very nice and the sun is pouring down, but no sign of any furniture. I ask someone handing out leaflets but he says he doesn't speak English and calls over his young female colleague who is a master of English but knows little about furniture. In Japan we have often found that the great English speakers are very nice and willing, but often lacking the answers we are seeking. When Linda called the help line for computers she easily found competent English speakers and good technicians, but never combined in one and the same person, often making it difficult to solve any problem.

Ultimately we do find some furniture but it is very arty and priced accordingly, so we decide to take a taxi to Chinatown for a walk around and some lunch. A ten minutes car ride for Y 980 takes us to the old Chinatown, which seems to be dominated by restaurants and other eateries. We find a nice- looking place, which isn't too full, and we sit down and I order a biro. We order a set lunch by pointing at the menu, having absolutely no clue what we might expect as the menu is all in

Japanese. As luck would have it, it all turns out to be an excellent mix of vegetables, meat and noodles, just what we were looking for. On our way back to the station we bought some tea and a few rolls of film, but other than that, nothing really tempted us. Ever since our first overseas move fifteen years ago and for each subsequent move, we have had several boxes labeled 'ornaments' and Linda is adamant we don't need more 'things.'

Back at Shibuya we look again at more shops and lo and behold, the third shop has just what we are looking for at one fifth of the price of the fancy design shops. A three-seater sofa, a small coffee table, a reading lamp, a small rice paper light and a little folding table for the balcony, all for Y 90,000 - delivery next Wednesday. Happy day! On our way back we walk through Yoyogi park and enjoy the many musicians that perform there every Saturday and Sunday. We must have walked five miles this day with no effort at all.

So what is the relevance of all this in relation to this space and the heading? Perhaps I have presented a few snapshots of life as I find it, and life as experienced and lived is always relevant - good experiences with good people is what you may wish for both friends and enemies. A lot of human effort is geared towards trying to secure just that for as many as possible. Like a bowl of cherries. Don't make it serious. It's too mysterious.

7. Judges

Rather similar to Joshua, Judges is a grim historical account of the expansion of Israel. Judges includes the story of Samson and Delilah.

The men of Judah attacked Jerusalem also and took it. They put the City to the sword and set it on fire. 1: 8
March on my soul; be strong! 5: 21
Since their land lacked nothing they were prosperous. 18: 7

Associations...

7 Judges

Hebron, Jericho, Gaza, when is it right to take a stand and fight?

Not for honor! I saw President Nixon on television talk about an honorable end to a most dishonorable war - the Vietnam War - when people were dying at the rate of thousands a day. Shockingly, he was holding peace up for honor! Whose honor? What honor? If you start to kill men for the ideas they have, for their political affiliations, or support undemocratic dictatorships because you think the dictator has a positive disposition to you and your policies, you are about as far removed from honor as you can get. The only honorable way to end a dishonorable venture is to repent and stop immediately. Unconditionally!

Not for territory! Expansion through force is just not acceptable. Today with 99 percent of all economic value being software, intelligence and knowledge it is particularly obvious that war for territorial gain is madness. Gaining territory by way of force is also not conducive to lasting peace and happiness. Violent territorial conflict runs the obvious risk of producing perpetual hostilities and misery for all. Sustainable solutions must be negotiated in good faith and agreed.

Not for loot! The conquistadors and their backers got away with it. The Vikings! The Mongols! Raping and pillaging. Thieving and raving. Indiscriminate murdering for gain! One of the great benefits with globalization and improved communication is that a win-lose strategy has become nigh impossible. Any other strategy than a win-win philosophy is obviously going to reduce the total wealth and happiness. Today with instant communication it is getting increasingly difficult to run foul play undetected anywhere in the world. Even if we have many difficult issues to address and progress around the globe, I believe there is greater justice and freedom from fear than ever before. We must keep talking, keep improving and keep reacting against criminal/narrow minded/egotistical behavior by individuals and by states.

For freedom! Yes, for freedom only. It may be justifiable to take up arms to protect our rights to make basic decisions concerning ourselves and for an independent and fair justice system. Even Saint Augustine suggests that to get rid of tyrannical oppression, force may well be a better alternative than obedience. Give me liberty or give me death. Once there is freedom, territory and other issues can be dealt with. Freedom of thought, freedom from oppression, freedom of movement, freedom of speech and freedom of press give you access to peaceful means to enjoy the world and to argue without fear and along democratic lines for change and improvement.

Freedom and security is not the same thing. They can be very much opposites. The bird in the cage has security - food and care in abundance - but lacking the most fundamental of rights; to make its own decisions, to spread its wings and go where it pleases. It has no freedom.

Judges, which holds a lot of mythical cruelty, making it perhaps interesting but not very easy to reconcile with the love teachings of the New Testament, has this lovely verse in 5:10 - 12.

"You who ride the white donkeys,
Sitting on your saddle blankets,
and you who walk along the road,
consider the voice of the singers,
at the watering places,
they recite the righteous acts
wake up wake up, break out in song."

Song and music has a tendency to soften and reconcile. Coming together in song and music produces in most people feelings of elation, relaxation and brotherhood. The book 'A People's Tragedy, A History of the Russian Revolution' by Orlando Figes has this interesting comment ascribed to Vladimir Lenin : "I can't listen to music too often' he once admitted after a performance of Bethoven's Appassionata Sonata. 'It makes me want to say kind, stupid things, and pat the heads of people. But now you have to beat them on the head, beat them without mercy.' Interesting!

Phone rings...do I want to play tennis?? Do I ever! I love it. In spite of the tropical heat in Singapore!

8. Ruth

Beautiful account of how Ruth was loyal to her mother-in-law and got rewarded!

Why have I found such favor in your eyes that you notice me - a foreigner? 2: 10

May the Lord repay you for what you have done! May you be richly rewarded by the Lord, the God of Israel, under whose wings you have come to take refuge! 2: 11

For the redemption and transfer of property to become final, one party took off his sandal and gave it to the other. This was the method of legalizing transactions in Israel. 4: 7

Associations...

8 Ruth

My father Georg's sister was Ruth. She died of tuberculosis nineteen years old in 1936, the year when Jesse Owen had his successful runs at the Berlin Olympics. It is less than one hundred years ago that death struck into every family around the world in the form of deceases that no one could control. To be a girl of only nineteen, all set to bloom, and be swept away like that is heart breaking. It still happens for various reasons but the likelihood is so much less due to the progress of medicine. Even if risks have declined I am not so sure that our worries have. The amount of worries may be constant or perhaps even increasing with growing affluence. There is more time to worry. This all has to be managed with wisdom and faith and love.

Georg, my father, lived to be seventy-nine. That is just over average life expectancy in Sweden. World life expectancy increased by twenty years or 50 % over the last century. It was less of an increase for Sweden which started out from a favorable position. Japan now tops the league with 84 years for women and 78 years for men. Still it was very sad to see him go. He was such a fine and wise person, always looking for the funny angle, always there to advice and support. Many of his contemporary friends are still around but I guess any year after 78 is a bonus. In fact any year is a bonus. We must learn to count our blessings and appreciate what we have rather than pity what isn't ours to have. Georg did that. Always accepted the inevitable, always kept his spirits high, always keen never to burden anyone.

When in younger day's I sometimes faced two job alternatives I asked him for advice he would say: 'Price 'em out!!' or 'Toss the coin, and if you don't like what you get, toss it again!' I am sure he never meant that money should be the sole decider but rather that the merits and growth potential in either situation should be assessed and compared. Even at the peak of my earnings he would send me some money now and then, just in case and also to achieve equal treatment between my two sisters and me. Never ever any burden, just an endless source of support and love!

He may have extended his life span a bit if he hadn't smoked so much, if he had nurtured some stronger interests and if he had focused a bit more on physical exercise. However, he was in charge of his own life, he lived a quality life surrounded by family and friends. Under such circumstances, who can complain about life ending. A good film or book is not praised for its length but for its quality and content. It is just that for those who remain behind, it seems such a void that someone you have respected and loved has moved on. In the book 'No Ordinary Times' about the years of FDR, his wife, Eleanor Roosevelt says upon her husbands death: "They are not dead who live in the lives they leave behind. In those whom they have blessed they live a life again."

For our father's funeral my sisters had arranged something quite unusual and beautiful. In the little chapel in Stockholm's western suburbs on a clear and cold November day 1999, they had invited a quartet of New Orleans jazz musicians who slowly and quietly played 'Just a Closer Walk with Thee' and a few other similar pieces. It just couldn't have been more beautiful and more fitting. I know that he would have loved the idea of bringing this spiritual music to all his congregated family and friends and prove how beautiful and positive a funeral can be. Thank you, Georg! May you be richly rewarded!

9. Samuel 1

Saul and Samuel! David and Goliath! Saul tries to kill David. David spares Saul's life. Saul takes his life. Grim and violent narrative throughout!

Hannah, why are you weeping? Why don't you eat? Why are you downhearted? Don't I mean more to you than ten sons? 1:8

I am a woman who is deeply troubled. I have not been drinking wine or beer. 1:15

She got a son and named him Samuel for she was heard of God. 1:20

It is not by strength that one prevails. Those who honor me I will honor, but those who despise me will be disdained.2: 30

We're in trouble, nothing like this has happened before.4: 7

What is wrong with the people? Why are they weeping? 11:5

If you persist in doing evil, both you and your king will be swept away. 12:25

Do what seems best to you. 14: 40.

When a lion or bear came and carried off a sheep from the flock I went after it, struck it and rescued the sheep from its mouth.17: 34-35.

David triumphed over the Philistine (Goliath, over nine feet tall 17:5) with a sling and a stone. 17:50.

Show kindness to your servant. 20:8

You are more righteous than I, he said. You have treated me well, but I have treated you badly. You have just now told me of the good you did to me. 24:17

Good health to you and your household! And good health to all that is yours! 25:6

Let no wrongdoing be found in you as long as you live 25:28

Associations...

9 First Samuel

Sometimes we are too keen and focused on some result and therefore it eludes us. Once we relax and count our blessings and put the importance of our objective in perspective, it is in fact easier to make good progress. Nothing is more important than to try to be a delight to our friends and ourselves. You will be loved more rather than less because of some little human shortcoming, subject that you don't allow it to make you lose joy and self-esteem. Life teaches us that flawless people are a myth; they just don't exist. Give love and you shall receive it.

Train your mind and judgment to make calls, to make decisions. You cannot play a game with anyone unless you play your part. If you try to play the other person's part, it's the end of the game. You have extinguished yourself and your role. Humans have a unique capability to collate a variety of information including reading moods and emotional currents. Delegating your right to have a view and make decisions, even to your spouse, is not conducive to developing integrity, self-respect and personal growth.

David beat Goliath. Small is beautiful. We see trends towards corporations getting larger and larger. At the same time there are more very small startups than ever. Each human being is unique and wants to be recognized for her uniqueness and to be respected as an individual. Democracy, justice and freedom are all designed to give the individual those qualities. If corporations, government or organizations get so large and powerful that the rights and influence of individuals - be they employees, customers or citizens in general - get lost or seriously compromised, then they are bound for decay and ultimately break-up.

To be successful on a large scale you must therefore nurture the health of your cells, you must ensure that they independently develop immunity to cloning and unethical manipulation. In the age of intellectual capital the individual and his or her motivation is key, and any growth in size must be commensurate with individual excitement, contentment and satisfaction. If you are big to the extent that you are dominant, you must be ultra cautious so you don't step over the line, causing redress from courts or international institutions. Size at some stage inevitably also restricts growth. Any size where the individual or individual's influence and enthusiasm get compromised is already too large. Sustainable growth is best achieved by way of growing healthy small cells.

Health and longevity requires three things: that you eat and drink with wisdom and moderation, avoiding excesses and also avoiding smoking; that you have some interest in life, something that makes you want to get up in the morning and live to see another day; and that you do physical exercises of some sort on a regular basis. Simple! Only three things to get right! You are already doing it? Fine! If not, please start now. Every delay will inevitably take its toll in quality and length of life.

10. Samuel 2

David king over Judah! War between the houses of David and Saul. David king over Israel! David defeats the Philistines. David takes Uriah's wife Batsheba and sends him to his death. David flees. David returns to Jerusalem.

Saul and Jonathan - in life they were loved and gracious, and in death they were not parted. They were swifter than eagles and they were stronger than lions. 1: 23

Oh daughters of Israel, weep for Saul, who clothed you in scarlet and finery, who adorned your garments with ornaments of gold. 1: 24

Be strong and brave 2: 7

David reigned over Israel, doing what was right and just for all his people. 8: 15

> *To the faithful you show yourself faithful,*
> *to the blameless you show yourself blameless,*
> *to the pure you show yourself pure*
> *but to the crooked you show yourself shrewd.*
> *You save the humble,*
> *but your eyes are on the haughty to bring them low. 22: 26 - 28*

Evil men are to be cast aside like thorns. 23: 6

Associations...

10 Second Samuel

So many fine little passages! I have tried to find them all but feel sure that in spite of reading the book attentively I may well have missed and overlooked some pearls. As it says elsewhere in the text, don't go over your tree twice; leave something for the hungry and the wayfarer. Perhaps it doesn't matter. We don't have to be complete. We don't have to be exact. All we need is enough pieces to paint the picture, to perceive what it looks like, how it all hangs together. We need to know when to stop without being too sketchy. If we wait until the research is complete, we will never move beyond the research. Great artists engage and involve your imagination. Without imagination and participation there is nothing of real value.

To repay a good turn with a good turn and to repay a bad turn with correctness is part of what Confucius taught. To minimize bad turns makes a lot of sense but is not necessarily natural. If we think about not rewarding evil with evil and remind ourselves of that frequently, turning the other cheek can be done and can also give a tremendous sense of satisfaction. Leo Tolstoy talks about the person who has been imprisoned for twenty eight years on false accusations, then finds himself in the same cell as his accuser, who at a pertinent moment he protects from death by not telling on him - that is life-changing and world improving behavior. Quite often the explanation for evil is that the culprit simply has never seen virtue and benevolence.

After ten years of virtually no economic growth Japan in the beginning of the 21st century needs reform and change. But everybody seems to look at the next person for this to happen. It isn't the next person that needs to initiate or implement change. It is you and I. For the next person we are the next person. We can't just look around and ask: "Where is the leader?" We must step up to the challenge and be the agent of change. We don't have to march in perfect order to the same tune. It is enough that we agree on the style of music and turn in small groups to better ways. Vested interests, excess discipline, fear of change, and education lacking in character formation may be some of the causes. These problems are not difficult to understand and quite possible to influence on a micro basis in our own jobs, families, schools etc. Let's read and write and discuss the issues at every opportunity and perhaps most importantly, try to role model the better way as we see it. This is leadership available to many if not all.

So will Japan pull it off? Yes, I think so. It just got a bit carried away with its own success, perhaps getting a bit arrogant in the process. History abounds with examples of similar stories. When things are going really well you need to take time out to understand why the progress may be deceptive. A saying I picked up during my army training is: "Efter segern, spänn hjälmen hårdare." After the victory, tighten the helmet. And a quote from the Chinese epic 'The Romance of the Three Kingdoms' refers: 'After fifteen successive victories, Wut'uku and the Rattan Army were greatly cheered and began to feel contempt for the enemy. The sixteenth day, they were utterly defeated!?' We are most vulnerable when things are going really well.

In the eighties I remember hearing stories about the Emperor's palace area in central Tokyo, having a higher real estate value than the state of California and the real estate value of Japan was two and a half times that of all of the United States. People were joking about it at gatherings and parties but why didn't anyone see the madness of it all? In many cases the new property values are twenty to thirty percent of previous fantasy values and of course that is very serious for over extended banks. And without healthy banks providing lubrication for the economy, a drawn out period of economic malfunctioning is inevitable.

Humility is perhaps the most valuable of all virtues and a prerequisite for love. One of the key messages of religion as I see it is to make it clear to humanity that we are all visitors and guests for a little while during our short lives, and that all the wonders of the world were not created by man. Regardless of your faith it is in place to take your hat off and say thank you for the opportunity.

Here my thoughts remind me of a beautiful passage in St Augustine's 'The City of Good' book twenty-second (the last book).

"How can I tell of the rest of creation, with all its beauty and utility, which the divine goodness has given to man to lease his eye and serve his purposes, condemned though he is, and hurled into these labors and miseries? Shall I speak of the manifold and various loveliness of sky, and earth, and sea; of the plentiful supply and wonderful qualities of the light; of sun, moon, and stars; of the shade of trees, of the colors and perfume of the flowers; of the multitude of birds, all differing in plumage and in song; of the variety of animals, of which the smallest in size are often the most wonder - the works of ants and bees astonishing us more than the huge bodies of whales? Shall I speak of the sea, which itself is so grand a spectacle, when it arrays itself as it were in vestures of various colors, now running through every shade of green, and again becoming purple or blue? Is it not delightful to look at it in storm, and experience the soothing complacency, which it inspires by suggesting that we ourselves are not tossed and shipwrecked? What shall I say of the numberless kinds of foods to alleviate hunger, and the variety of seasonings to stimulate appetite which are scattered everywhere by nature, and for which we are not indebted to the art of cookery? How grateful is the alternation of day and night! How pleasant the breezes that cool the air! How abundant the supply of clothing furnished us by trees and animals! Who can enumerate the blessings we enjoy?"

11. Kings 1

David makes his son Solomon King.

The King said, "This woman says my son is alive and your son is dead" while that woman says, "No! Your son is dead and mine is alive". Then the King said, "Bring me a sword." So they brought a sword for the king. He then gave an order: "Cut the living child in two and give half to the one and half to the other."

The woman whose son was alive was filled with compassion for her son and said to the king, "Please, my lord, give her the living baby! Don't kill him!" But the other said. "Neither I nor you shall have him. Cut him in two!" Then the King gave this ruling: "Give the living baby to the first woman. Do not kill him: she is his mother."

When all Israel heard the verdict the king had given, they held the king in awe, because they saw that he had wisdom from God to administer justice. 3: 23 - 28

One who puts on his armor should not boast like one who takes it off. 20: 11

Associations...

11 First Kings

Why is it that we can make such major issue of the smallest thing and allow it to consume us, when for any onlooker the lack of proportions appear utterly bizarre. It certainly has happened to me a couple of times in life - many years ago, I am pleased to say - and in hindsight the emotions seem exaggerated, foolish and unfounded.

More often than not aggravation is driven by envy or fear, sometimes by arrogance and a rigid view on the need for justice. Both envy and fear, in turn are caused by too much focus on the self, and an inability to put oneself and one's issues in perspective. Eleanor Roosevelt has been quoted as saying: "no one can insult me without my consent". Tacitus wrote in the first century: "The divine Julius endured insults and let them be. This could be interpreted as wise policy and not forbearance. For things unnoticed are forgotten; resentment confers status on them."

On the radio last night I heard of a court case in the UK concerning the height of a hedge. The court case took five years out of the contestants' lives and cost one hundred and fifty thousand pounds. Surely all involved would rather have this process undone and would regret it ever started. Technically arbitration is the better way for conflict resolution. Better still is if the conflict isn't allowed to rise so out of proportion. We must stop and ask ourselves, does it really matter? Positive excitement - get as much of it as you can! Negative excitement - try to avoid it. It is a poison for you as well as for those around you. Usually, in the end, the one that keeps his cool wins. Key is not so much justice in small things as how such things can be managed without undue agony. Proverbs 26:4 has a useful guiding principle: - Do not answer a fool according to his folly, or you will be like him yourself.

My own experiences are related to hostility in the work place. Someone thinks you are in his or her way and tries to undermine your position. This is probably not uncommon and the best way to approach it is to do a good job, keep your spirits high, and make an extra effort to show good will. There is a more than even probability that the problem will go away, or at least diminish over time. If you lose your temper or good humor, you have less of a chance of coming through unscathed. My experience suggests that the remedy for these situations is to try as best as possible to ensure you have nothing to reproach yourself for. Cicero in the second century wrote: 'Nothing is more to be praised, nothing more worthy of a great and splendid man, than to be easily appeased and forgiving.'

Good intentions only come to fruition when followed by good actions. Good spirits is a virtue whereas arrogance is a vice. Examples abound in sports and warfare of arrogance preceding fall. You are the most vulnerable when you have done something well. You think it is easy. In fact nothing is so easy that you can continue to succeed without humbly applying all your faculties and efforts. Outstanding performance requires outstanding commitment. The more we excel, the more humbly we should behave.

12. Kings 2

The Lord's Judgment on Ahaziah, healing of the water, The widow's oil, the Shunammite's son restored to life, Feeding of a hundred, Famine in Besieged Samaria, Jehu anointed King of Israel, Jezebel killed, Israel exiled because of sin, Jerusalem's deliverance foretold, The fall of Jerusalem.

Associations...

12 Second Kings

This is a very interesting read in many ways but rather void of love and any hints at good conduct. It illustrates that war and deceit leads to war and deceit and that the only hope for a better life is that the vicious circle be broken. To a large extent conditions have improved over the millennia, but we still have the Middle East Crisis, probably the most serious conflict area the world currently faces. Others are Kashmir, Sri Lanka, The Balkans, The Koreas, Taiwan, and Northern Ireland besides a number of more local conflicts. And yet these are exceptions rather than the rule and more people than ever live away from real tangible fear. But the media like vultures hover over the world twenty four hours a day to find something grisly to report. Media seems to thrive on violence and disruption calling it 'breaking news' - something that legitimately should be in everyone's living room. Then of course you don't have to see and listen to the news all the time. At the same time, we do need to beware of the little skirmishes as they carry within them the nucleus and potential for a devastating wildfire.

Through my window I see it is now raining. Not very heavily, just a light, cleansing, life-giving autumn rain! Good I took the dog out early before the rain started. And the little radio cum cassette player I bought in Akihabara for my language practice is giving me the Neujahrs konzerten by Wiener Philarmoniker - making me feel like dancing, waltzing. Not a bad setting for some positive reflection and thought.

Having read again First Kings and Second Kings the epic 'The Romance of the Three Kingdoms' keep reappearing in my mind! This book was written in China in roughly the same time period as the books of the Old Testament. Covering thirteen hundred pages it just about equals the Bible in size as well. The happenings are not that dissimilar - war flowing back and forth, a world full of deceit, cruelty and quest for power, but still somewhere a glimmer of hope of better things to come by one or two outstanding people rising above self serving and personal enrichment, seeking to achieve providence, peace and happiness for the many victims of ambition gone astray.

From this book I quote a few lines: "On the march, restrain your men from plunder and license lest the ordinary people be against us. Wherever you halt, be compassionate and kindly and do not give way to anger and flog your men. The prudent bird chooses its perch and the wise man his master. He who offends against heaven has no one to pray to. The will of heavens does not follow the way of mortals, but seeks the virtuous. He who accords with the Heavens shall flourish, while he who opposes shall be destroyed. How can one stand in this world if one forgets duty through fear? I refuse to risk the loss of the confidence and the trust of the world for a trifling advantage. Improve learning and hide the sword; establish schools and so give people the blessings of peace."

To me it is quite amazing how similar moral concepts seemed to have grown contemporaneously around much of the known world about two thousand five hundred years ago; the Greeks, Biblical authors, Persians and Indians, Confucius and Mencius. As if people around the world then realized quite suddenly that without some 'proper conduct' the harvest and the spoils of victory often are seeds of self-destruction. Living a lie is false heaven. Progress at other peoples' expense is frail and deceptive. The parallels to modern day are only too obvious. Reading some of this fine historic literature gives cause for reflection. And it is all there. In spite of our modern day obsession with change, on the most interesting of subjects - the way people interact and communicate, live and love - there is not much that our early predecessors didn't consider and contemplate. Mencius and St Augustine continue to be highly relevant.

13. Chronicles 1

Essentially chronicles is a long account of how various people are related, who is a son of whom etc. There is David's Psalm of thanks / God's promise to David / David's Prayer / David's Victories / Preparations for the Temple /

Consider now for the Lord has chosen you to build a temple as a sanctuary. Be strong and do the work. 28: 10

David also said to Salomon his son, "Be strong and courageous, and do the work. Do not be afraid or discouraged". Every willing man, skilled in any craft will help you in all the work. The officials and all the people will obey your every command. 28: 20-21

Associations...

13 First Chronicles

A few thousand years or 30 - 50 generations may seem a long period of time. But in light of the estimated 450 million years that life has existed on our planet, and even in light of the history of man of say ten million years, it is all very recent. Key inventions like farming and irrigation freed people's time up so as to allow for more thinking, painting and writing. In spite of our formidable population growth, a greater portion of the world's population than ever, live in freedom of fear and hunger. This is no small feat.

In addition people live longer and longer and in what we call the industrialized world the population is about to, or already has, stopped growing in numbers. This provides a unique opportunity to make lasting improvements in the quality of life for all. But the raising of living standards in the most populous areas must be managed carefully as humanity cannot cope with a world that pollutes to the same relative extent as some western countries, particularly America and Europe, do. Thus pollution free growth is an absolute must for retaining the highest quality of life. It can and must be achieved.

The fear that environmental concerns may slow growth are misguided, because there can be no sustainable growth other than that which is consistent with keeping the environment healthy. All that happens if you try to grow faster is that a liability builds up which over time needs to be reckoned with and paid for. Unfortunately traditional accounting doesn't take into consideration the using up of fresh air and water and other products of nature. However, at the current world population level, there is no resource that even comes close to being infinite. Preservation requires monitoring and management. All inputs are in fact finite and we cannot continuously tap more out of the system than the system can reproduce. Any attempt to overtax the system is highly unethical as well as unsustainable, and means reduced room for quality of life for our children and grand children.

In the savings and capital formation markets there are now available a number of 'products' and funds that represent 'ethical investment'. Some say that fund managers should look for returns only. This may be so, but the returns will not be sustainable for business that acts without due regard to the health and survival of the local or world community. My prediction is that 'ethical investment' will grow to dominate and finally exclude any other investment. And corporations will be well advised to make a commitment to, and annually account for, how they ensure all their activity is ethically sound. The opposite to ethical investment and ethical conduct is unethical investment and unethical conduct. Unethical and environmentally oblivious investment or business activity runs an ever-increasing risk of being subjected to crippling legal action and/ or consumer boycott. Small business will be checked by local communities and large business will be checked by the web-networked world community. Which saver, investor or fund manager in his right mind can afford to run low on commitment to ethics and the environment?

Business will be required to make more effort to discern whether earnings are quality earnings or mere quantity. The author Jonathan Sachs points out 'If we want to pick the flowers we must help tend to the garden. We can change the world if we can change ourselves.' Be strong and courageous and do the work.

14. Chronicles 2

Salomon builds the Temple / Salomon's Splendour / Salomon's Death / Shishak attacks Jerusalem / Joash repairs the Temple / The fall of Jerusalem

Forgive, and deal with each man according to all he does, since you know his heart (for you alone know the hearts of men), so that they will fear you and walk in your ways all the time they live in the land that you gave our fathers. 6:31

Associations...

14 Second Chronicles

In light of the events of the 11th September 2001, just about two months ago, there is an intense desire to understand Islam and its relation to other religions and to establish if one is intrinsically evil whereas other religions are good. This tension had been brewing for some time, in some ways since the life of the prophet Mohammad around 600 A.D. but intensifying more recently after an earlier period of relative harmony. Six months ago I read the Koran to try to improve my understanding.

All three Middle East founded religions have a lot in common and, as I understand it, are sharing the same God. This makes it almost incomprehensible that so much of hate and atrocities have taken place in the name of these religions. These evils have absolutely nothing to do with religion, which by design is there to promote brotherhood, (and sisterhood) compassion and caring. But people who indiscriminately believe everything they read in these 'Holy texts' are facing many contradictions and irreconcilable values.

How can a book be holy? How can a building be holy? How can a person be holy? Isn't it rather the spirit, the flame, the conduct and the borderless, all inclusive love and compassion, supported by the doctrine of all religion, that is divine? The greatest value lies in the software, not in the hardware! Looking up the word 'holy' in the dictionary the explanations confirm the extreme range of its meanings from 'infinitely good and virtuous' via 'dedicated to the service of God' to being awesome, frightening or beyond belief' and 'filled with superhuman, and potentially fatal power.'

As an aside, when I was on a jury for a rape case in New Zealand some years ago, I and eleven colleagues were asked to swear on the bible with another option being committing to tell the truth. According to the principles I espouse, I alone felt it natural to choose the latter. The accused insisted he never had sex with the girl and forensic tests said conclusively that he was the father of an aborted fetus. Most of my colleagues wanted to acquit as not guilty. And the group included four women. How did they reason? Did they consider her partly guilty for having had some wine with him that evening? Did they consider him punished enough by living with the uncertainty of a prison sentence for one year? Or did they feel it impossible to call beyond reasonable doubt? It left me puzzled.

Religion, it seems to me, is there to protect us from evil, not to cause evil. There may well be evil, self-serving, oppressive and narrow-minded interpretations but the religions as such, as I see it, are not evil. Most people are not evil; they are good. They want peace and prosperity for themselves and their kin, and once enlightened they know that this is best achieved by non-discriminatory all inclusive care and compassion.

Let us look at the beauty of some of the lines from the Koran: "God desires your well-being, not your discomfort; Be charitable, God loves the charitable; Women shall with justice have rights similar to those exercised against them; Men shall be rewarded according to their deeds and women shall be rewarded according to their deeds; Do not forget to show kindness to each other; He untied your hearts so you are now brothers through his grace; If relatives, orphans, or needy men are present at the division of an inheritance, give them too a share of it and speak kind words to them; Give just weight and full measure; Help one another in what is good and pious, not in what is wicked and sinful. Whoever killed a human being shall be considered having killed all mankind; Be they men or women, the hypocrites are all alike. They enjoin what is evil, forbid what is just, and tighten their fists; In no way does God wrong mankind, but men wrong themselves; He created spouses from among yourselves that you may live in peace with them, and planted love and kindness in your hearts."

And I come back to what Tolstoy has Jesus say: 'I don't ask you to believe in me, I ask you to try to understand what I am saying.' You must espouse the divine message. The Kingdom of God - the ultimate caring, compassionate and loving society - can only come from within each and every one of us. Embrace the good and hold on to it with all your might. Amen.

III Ezra through Proverbs with Associations

15. Ezra

This is what Cyrus, king of Persia says: "The Lord the God of heaven, has given me all the kingdoms of the earth and he has appointed me to build a temple for him at Jerusalem in Judah. Anyone of his people among you - may his God be with him, and let him go up to Jerusalem in Judah and build the temple of the Lord, the God of Israel, the God who is in Jerusalem. And the people of any place where survivors may now be living are to provide him with silver and gold, with goods and livestock, and with freewill offerings for the temple of God in Jerusalem" 1: 2 - 5

/Rebuilding the Altar / Rebuilding the Temple / Opposition to the Rebuilding / Ezra's Prayer About Intermarriage /

Associations...

15 Ezra

Jerusalem is not far from 10,000 year old Jericho. Jerusalem was first referred to in Egyptian literature 4,000 years ago. It was captured by David 3000 years ago and destroyed by Titus 2,000 years ago. Crusaders invaded it 1,000 years ago. Jerusalem has been subject to innumerable wars and earthquakes; fifty major sieges, eighteen reconstructions and eleven changes of religion. And it is a top agenda news item in the year 2000 A.D in respect of crucial negotiations for lasting peace between Israel and Palestine. Such a fantastic place filled with layers and layers of history, holy to three religions and perhaps to two billion people. As the whole city rests on ancient predecessors it is impossible to uncover all hidden treasures. The four parts of the city inside the wall - Armenian, Greek, Jewish, and Moslem Quarters - show how it has been multicultural through the millennia. Accessed through eight gates; the colorful and bristling Damascus Gate, the impressive Jaffa Gate, the well guarded Dung Gate leading to the Dome on the Rock and the Wailing Wall. View it from the top of the Mount of Olives in the late afternoon and then stroll down the Mount slowly through Gethsemane with the 2000 year old olive trees and then up the hill through the St Stephen's/ Lion Gate along the Via Dolorosa and just absorb the atmosphere. It grips you like a whisper and a breeze and integrates the passage of history with your body and soul.

With or without any agreement it must be kept open and available for the world citizenry including all the local tribes and peoples. It has no significant economic value. It does have an immeasurable spiritual value to mankind. Spiritual values cannot be claimed, restricted or fenced in. They must, by their very nature, flow freely through walls, bodies and hearts. Perhaps there is a solution in making it an open city, a bit like the Vatican, with its own government and policing where all can meet and live in peace. The majority of those immediately concerned no doubt want a fair agreement with universal access. What stand in its way are hatred, suspicion and fear of rioting and violence - all contrary to the fundamental teachings of religion. Obaidah di Bertinoro wrote in 1487: "In Jerusalem there is not one wise and sensible man who knows how to deal affably with his fellow man; all are ignorant misanthropes, intent only on gain." Interesting! Judging from history, a lasting solution looks like an illusion.

Yet I remain optimistic.

Why? Because of the strong economic dependence of Palestinians on neighboring Israel and the realization in Israel that an open sore always runs the risk of converting into lethal infection. Education among interested peoples is continuing its spread and penetration. Interconnectedness of today's world means that land boundaries are surpassed and a free flow of communications and contacts is unstoppable. International pressure! It is in the interest of the whole world to manage tension and avoid open full-scale conflict as in this day and age there can be no winners of conflicts by war. And as A.N.

Wilson says in 'The Wealth and Poverty of Nations:' "In this world the optimists have it, not because they are always right, but because they are positive, and that is the way of achievement, correction, improvement and success. Educated, eyes-open optimism pays; pessimism can only offer the empty consolation of being right."

Jerusalem is a city of history, religion, mystique and eternity. It is there for all mankind to revere.

16. Nehemiah

Nehemiah Inspects Jerusalem's Walls / Builders of the Wall / Opposition to the Rebuilding / The Completion of the Wall / Ezra Reads the Law / Dedication of the wall of Jerusalem /

Come let us rebuild the wall of Jerusalem. 2: 17

So we rebuilt the wall till all of it reached half its height, for the people worked with all their heart. 4:6

Some of our daughters have already been enslaved, but we are powerless, because our fields and our vineyards belong to others. 5: 5

Let the exacting of usury stop! Give back to them immediately their fields, vineyards, olive groves and houses, and also the usury you are charging them - the hundredth part of the money, grain, new wine and oil. 5: 11

At the dedication of the wall of Jerusalem, the Levites were sought out from where they lived and were brought to Jerusalem to celebrate joyfully the dedication with songs of thanksgiving and with the music of cymbals, harps and lyres. The singers also were brought together from the region around Jerusalem. 12: 27 – 29

Associations...

16 Nehemiah

When people put their heart into what they do, no achievement is out of reach. When it feels to those who participate like a blessing to be able to work a few more hours and do a little bit more, then you know that a strong sense of purpose and a unifying team spirit is there.

Mobilizing the will, making the discretionary energy come to the fore, finding and defining the cause that moves men and women and puts the soul on fire - that is leadership at its best.

A precondition for such divine effort is that the outcome and results are shared fairly and that all contributors are recognized as unique human beings of whom each and everyone has an equal desire and entitlement to growth, development, love and happiness. Any exploitation can only long term end with a reaction, a crash. To tread an exploitative course is nothing short of foolishness and madness - greed trying to win over love. The very definition of humankind is such that exploitation can never succeed.

In the business world we must stop saying 'this is business,' as if business can be run in a vacuum, free from any obligation to respect, love and integrity and serving mankind. It cannot. Forced and voluntary transparency today means than any shady purpose or course is doomed and set to fail and come to an end. It is simply unsustainable. People are wise to stay away from such enterprise, whether in the capacity as labor, customer, subcontractor or investor. This is already starting to happen and will be more commonplace in future.

And work should not necessarily be seen as the end of human life. It is part of the need and desire to feel useful, appreciated and contributing. Part of happiness is effort and this effort needs to be for some other than merely self-serving cause. If we work for ourselves only, we never get that ultimate reward of knowing that we have helped someone along, i.e. building friendships, goodwill and credit. Proper understanding of these issues holds the ultimate possibility to mobilize energy, commitment and joy. On the joy of living for others, Tolstoy says in "What Men Live By" written 1881: "I have learned that every man lives, not through care of himself, but by love. I have learned that God does not wish men to live each for himself, and therefore He has not revealed to them what they each need for themselves, but He wishes them to live in union, and therefore He has revealed to them what is necessary for each and for all together. I have learned that it is only in appearance that they are kept alive through care for themselves, but that in reality they are kept alive through love. He who dwelleth in love dwelleth in God, and God in him, for God is love."

And profitable activity needs to be interwoven with non-profitable activity. By traditional accounting standards, profitable means materially rewarding whereas non-profitable means benefiting the soul. But if the soul is the ultimate motivator and driver of commitment and energy, soul related activity has the potential to be tremendously profitable.

Celebrate joyfully with the music of cymbals, harps and lyres. Bring the singers into it as well. Joy and music unites and moves man. Unity and action are cornerstones in any successful undertaking.

17. Esther

Esther made queen of Persia / Esther's Request to the King / The King's Edict on Behalf of the Jews / Purim Celebrated /

This is what happened during the time of Xerxes who, from his citadel of Susa, ruled over 127 provinces stretching from India to Cush. 1: 1–2

The royal wine was abundant, in keeping with the king's liberality. 1: 7

He proclaimed a holiday throughout the provinces and distributed gifts with royal liberality. 2: 18

Since it was customary for the king to consult experts in matters of law and justice, he spoke with the wise men that understood the times and were closest to the king. 1: 13

This advice appealed to the king and he followed it. 2: 4

The girl Hadassah, who was also known as Esther, was lovely in form and features. 2: 7

If it pleases the king, she said, and if he regards me with favor and thinks it the right thing to do, and if he is pleased with me, let an order be written overruling the dispatches that Haman son of Hammedatha, the Agagite, devised and wrote to destroy the Jew's in all the king's provinces. 8: 5

The Jews who were in the king's provinces, assembled to protect themselves and get relief from their enemies. They killed seventy-five thousand of them but did not lay their hands on the plunder. This happened on the thirteenth day of the month of Adar, and on the fourteenth they (14th June) rested and made it a day of feasting and joy. 9: 16 -17

Purim Celebrated. (The casting of the lot) The Jews in Susa, however, had assembled on the thirteenth and fourteenth, and then on the fifteenth they rested and made it a day of feasting and joy. That is why rural Jews - those living in villages - observe the fourteenth of the month of Adar as a day of joy and feasting, a day for giving presents to each other. 9: 18 – 19

Associations...

17 Esther

Esther was lovely in form and features. Though not very many words of description, she is easy to visualize. Given that she was Xerxes' pick from a huge empire she must have been something extraordinary. And she had a personality and loyalty to her origins, to match her beauty. Beauty is so much more than what meets the eye; it is countenance, sparkle and zest for life. It is broadmindedness and the ability to love and ignite a flame. No doubt she had it all. I have been blessed with three sons but no daughter, but if I had one, I would be delighted to have called her Esther. Thank heavens for little girls.

Xerxes listened. Although a man of immense authority and power he was humble and wise enough to debate ideas and compare his thinking to that of other trusted confidantes. How can we ever get people issues right if we rely solely on our own observations? Most issues are in fact people issues in as far as most issues concern people, or they wouldn't be issues. When we say that a large company has, say, 50% staff costs, this is always an understatement, as the bulk of the remainder is also staff related. For most goods and services more than 90 percent of the price is value added by humans in one way or another. And all customers and shareholders are people, whether acting for themselves, or through attorney. Great leaders have always relied on counsel of trusted people. Dictators and tyrants have not. The more you dominate, the more you suppress others' views and therefore risk omitting something essential.

History is full of examples of hidden agendas, trickery, and thievery. This has never provided sustainable benefit for anyone. Gain built on illicit means will forever be exposed to similar tactics being contemplated to reverse the flow of fortunes. A win - lose approach all too often leads to a 'lose – lose' outcome. With the whole world currently covered by satellite cameras and journalists, any large-scale wrongdoing or devious dealing is likely to be noted and condemned. This is one of the positives of increased interconnectedness and globalization.

But if I am too open, others may steel my ideas or I might be considered a fool. Fret not. If you talk to a number of people about your thinking the likelihood that you will come out richer and wiser by far outweighs any risk of having your idea copied or stolen. The process also generates friends and a potential that others feel involved in what you are doing and thus wishes for your success. What could be more fertile for progress than to have it desired by many, rather than be secretive and give the impression that you are working for yourself only.

If you are pursuing what you think is good for fellow men and women in general, that is a very sound and simple principle, which is easy to keep in mind. If you try to measure everything you do against its usefulness for mankind you know both when to praise and reprimand. And perhaps more importantly, you know how to choose your counsel. Beware of any counsel who is not committed to virtue and displaying trust and loyalty. The most intelligent person in the world would be of no use to you unless you know and respect what he or she values and you can trust his or her intent.

You should have the confidence to level with others, to show your open palms and to say: this is what I think; please tell me if you see it any differently? Ignatius Loyola advises that when we have stated our view, we add as calmly and unpretentiously as possible the rider 'salvo meliori iudicio', i.e. unless someone knows better.

Beware of flattery, especially if you carry high rank. From Machiavelli's The Prince, I quote: "There is no way of guarding against flattery but by letting it be seen that you take no offence in hearing the truth. And with the counselors collectively, and with each of them separately, his bearing should be such, that each and all of them may know that the more freely they declare their thoughts the better they will be liked. Good counsels have their origin in the leader, and not the prudence of the leader in wise counsel. It is important to be on friendly footing with your people and in all your actions try to inspire a sense of greatness and goodness."

Yes, this is from the Prince by Machiavelli, a book and an author that perhaps undeservedly has acquired a reputation for harshness, when all the author is trying to do, in my humble opinion, is give good advice as to princely conduct that achieves harmony and longevity in times of lawlessness and political instability.

18. Job

Those who plough evil and those who sow trouble reap it. 4: 8
Resentment kills a fool, and envy slays the simple. 5: 2

For hardship does not spring from the soil, nor does trouble sprout from the ground. 5: 6

Your beginnings will seem humble, so prosperous will your future be. 8: 7

For we were born only yesterday and know nothing, and our days on earth are but a shadow. 8: 9

Surely God does not reject a blameless man and strengthen the hands of evil-doers. 8:20

You gave me life and showed me kindness, and in your providence watched over my spirit. 10: 12

A witless man can no more become wise than a wild donkey's colt can be born a man. 11: 12

Is not wisdom found among the aged? Does not long life bring understanding? 12: 12

Only a few years will pass before I go on the journey of no return. 16: 22

The righteous will hold to their ways, and those with clean hands will grow stronger. 17: 9

I will never admit you are in the right; till I die, I will not deny my integrity. I will maintain my righteousness and never let go of it; my conscience will not reproach me as long as I live. 27: 5 - 6

Where can wisdom be found? Where does understanding dwell? The price of wisdom is beyond rubies. The topaz of Cush cannot compare with it; it cannot be bought with pure gold. 28: 18 - 19

But it is the spirit in the man, the breath of the Almighty that gives him understanding. It is not only the old who are wise, not only the aged who understand what is right. 32: 9

The ear tests words as the tongue tests food. Let us discern for ourselves what is right; let us learn together what is good. 34: 3 - 4

Associations...

18 Job

You gave me life and showed me kindness. Friendship is by far the best currency in which to measure wealth. You cannot accidentally lose it. It is not depleted by corrosion, inflation, tax or exploitation. It is the best medicine and support for all sorts of hardships. It is a remedy for loneliness, quoted as the single biggest social problem in western countries. The building blocks to gain friendship are care, affection and love. Showing an interest in other people, helping in any way you can. Trying to ease other people's problems also helps you see how small your own problems really are, putting yourself and your direct interests in perspective. Avoid getting attached to hardware, i.e. house, car, boat and whatever, as software, i.e. human interaction and building friendships, in the long run will prove infinitely more important for health and happiness.

It is true. Undue advantage becomes disadvantage. Stealing or betting sharply against the odds to win will neither make you rich nor happy. You may get away with it, but if you do, there is a more than even chance that you will feel encouraged, continuing with higher stakes. No one is lucky in the long run. Ultimately it is hard work and thorough analysis paired with a helpful attitude, which pay rewards. And mistreating others to get your own way and advantage is highly likely to end up by those others using their best endeavors to have you fall flat on your face. Serves you right too. Reciprocity works both in the positive and negative. Sooner or later you will make that mistake that allows people to get the last laugh. If not, you have to be so cautious and suspicious that all the fizz goes out of your life. The examples abound. The remedy is genuine generosity, care and affection. This is the stuff that keeps you in credit and reduces worry and provides a solid base for the pursuit of happiness.

'Only a few years will pass until I go on the journey of no return'. Human life is finite. Tomorrow never comes. We must use this knowledge to live our lives wisely and learn to appreciate the present. Your opportunity to make a difference will gradually dissipate. The biggest difference most of us can make is making life a little bit more pleasant and easier for our fellow travelers. This is incidentally what leadership and service is all about. The biggest leader of all "came to serve and not to be served." Matt: 20:28. The more the opportunity to serve is grasped, the better the universal quality of life.

Diluting your credibility and good will can be detrimental to future business. Either you are trying to contribute to a better order of things in good faith and adding value, or you are a parasite and a con. The choice is yours. Good and evil. One way can be sustainable, the other cannot. As an employee, as a customer or as an investor or regulator the preference and choice between the one and the other should be all too obvious. The alternative to ethical investment is unethical investment. Which approach do you prefer?

Either you have a view or you don't. If you find that you don't have a view on anything, you are loosing your humanity. 'Cogito, ergo sum.' Rene' Descartes said it. 'I think therefore I am'. He is also ascribed the saying: 'Man is not a means to an end, he is himself the end.' Don't just do as you are told. Robots are designed to follow instructions. Humans are equipped to do better than that. By using our brains we can and must try to add value and soul, interpolate, invent and innovate. Too many people in the corporate world, in government and large organizations simply go with the flow, unwilling to take a stand, afraid to rock the boat. What a waste of potential. What a sad state of affairs. If you don't have the courage to speak your mind, you will soon be out of it, you will loose it; Loose your mind! Let us discern for ourselves what is right; let us learn together what is good.

'Wisdom lies not in knowledge but in the pursuit of knowledge,' as per Socrates. Being is an illusion, only becoming is real! The world is dynamic and our aspirations must also be dynamic to be in harmony with the environment - learning new things, making new experiences, growing friendships and extending love further. Fear is self-perpetuating and so is freedom from fear. 'Cowards die many times before their deaths; the valiant never taste death but once' as per Shakespeare.

19. Psalms

This book contains one hundred and fifty Psalms essentially defining goodness and wickedness in quite poetic language. This is the longest book of the bible and in my view one of the finest.

Blessed is the man who does not walk in the counsel of the wicked… He is like a tree planted by streams of water, which yields its fruit in season and whose leaf does not wither. Whatever he does prospers. 1:1 - 6

He whose walk is blameless and who does what is righteous, who speaks the truth from his heart and who has no slander on his tongue, who does his neighbor no wrong and casts no slur on his fellow man…. He who does these things will never be shaken. 15: 1 - 5

You turned my wailing into dancing; you removed my sackcloth and clothed me with joy, that my heart may sing to you and not be silent…. 30: 11 - 12

No king is saved by the size of his army; no warrior escapes by his great strength. 33: 16

Better the little that the righteous have than the wealth of many wicked; for the power of the wicked will be broken. 37: 16 - 17

For all can see that wise men die; the foolish and the senseless alike perish and leave their wealth to others. 49: 10

Do not be overawed when a man grows rich when the splendor of his house increases, for he will take nothing with him when he dies, his splendor will not descend with him. 49: 16 - 18

On my bed I will remember you; I think of you through the watches of the night. Because you are my help, I sing the shadow of your wings. My soul clings to you; your right hand upholds me. 63: 6 - 8

May the nations be glad and sing for joy. 67: 4

So teach us to count our days that we may gain a wise heart. 90: 12

Even in darkness light dawns for the upright, for the gracious and compassionate and righteous man. God will come to him who is generous and lends freely, who conducts his affairs with justice. 112:4-5

Associations...

19 Psalms

He is like a tree planted in streams of water, which yields its fruit in season and whose leaf does not wither - he makes me lie down in green pastures besides quiet waters, restoring my soul - you turned my wailing into dancing and clothed me with joy - whoever of you who loves life and desires to see many good days, seek peace and pursue it - we meditate on your unfailing love - a pure heart and a steadfast spirit - I sing the shadows of your wings - my soul clings to you - may the nations be glad and sing for joy - have nothing to do with evil - compassionate and gracious, slow to anger abounding in love - generous and lending freely, conduct your affairs with justice.

What is poetic, good and beautiful not only survives repetition; it thrives on it. One hundred and twenty three words from one hundred and fifty paragraphs of Psalms contain almost everything you need to observe about conduct, ethics and values.

Lying down in green pastures besides quite waters restoring you soul! Is this not the epitome of youth, happy and excited about life and the many discoveries and pleasures yet to come? The unknown creates excitement and a feeling that the best is yet to happen. Today is the most beautiful present. We are often prone to seek security, and to eliminate risk and surprise, perhaps forgetting that the unchallenging secure life isn't worth living. It is only the realization that things may well go wrong that makes us thrive on the now and praise the day, which gives us so much. This is not pessimistic. Perhaps it is romantic dreaming, but why not? If you cannot dream, if you cannot feel the romance in the air, what can you feel? Seeking love and finding it in different clothing is itself a worthwhile and exciting course, a relationship and friendship waiting to happen. Few people talk about love. All seek it out. Love is never inappropriate. Love is life. Without love there is.......

The soul seems to have disappeared from many a modern work place. Why is that? Is it because it cannot be quantified? Perhaps! But we are pretty basic if we cannot recognize value that cannot be measured. The biggest single value of any company is its good will value, its potential to do well whether realized or not. No good will value - no company, at least no viable company. If the market value of a company is twice book, it means that the value of the spirit existing between staff, suppliers and customers and others is at least as big as the value of all capital goods employed. In the e-commerce sector the terrific values are often nothing but soul, i.e. an estimate of the potential of all soft and immeasurable ingredients.

The biggest single value of an individual is love, the ability, through compassion, to show appreciation and give a degree of comfort and that is immeasurable and thus impossible to price. Customers have soul and our children have soul. All our staff are also customers and children. They have soul as well, and when the soul is catered for, nourished and looked after, the future potential is without limit. What has a man gained if he wins the whole world but loses his soul? Those who forget to nourish the soul live dangerously and haven't really understood the human condition.

May nations be glad and sing! Great progress has been made. And yet there is so much more to do, so many people still hungry and oppressed. Material wealth without some peace and tranquility in which to enjoy it is meaningless. Louis XV of France, President Suharto of Indonesia. The late Shah Reza of Iran. The late Tsar Nicholai. They had everything. They had nothing. Assets without compassion and justice are like gold ore on the moon, infinitely less worth than friendship and freedom from fear.

Zest for life with the words of Psalms
Like a tree planted
in streams of water,
Yielding its fruit in season,
Whose leaf will not wither

Whoever of you love life
Will see many good days
If you seek peace

Turn wailing into dancing
Cloth yourself with joy
May your heart be pure
And your spirit steadfast

Compassionate and gracious,
Slow to anger, abounding in love
Generous and lending freely,
conducting all affairs with justice

Committed to unfailing love
I sing the shadows of your wings
May all nations be glad and sing for joy
Zest for life, my soul clings to you

20. Proverbs

Such is the end of all who go after ill-gotten gain; it takes away the lives of those who get it. 1: 19

Let love and faithfulness never leave you; bind them around your neck, write them on the tablet of your heart. Then you will win favor and a good name. 3: 3 - 4

Do not forsake wisdom and, she will protect you;
love her and she will watch over you.
Wisdom is supreme, therefore get wisdom,
Though it cost you all you have, get understanding.
Esteem her and she will exalt you; embrace her, and she will honor you. 4: 6 - 8

Let your eyes look straight ahead, fix your gaze directly before you.
Make level paths for your feet and take only ways that are firm.
Do not swerve to the right or the left; keep your foot from evil. 4: 25-27

The wise in heart accepts commands, but a chattering fool comes to ruin. The man of integrity walks securely, but he who takes crooked paths will be found out. 10: 8 - 9

Hatred stirs up dissension, but love covers over all wrongs. 10: 12

The integrity of the upright guides them, but the unfaithful are destroyed by their duplicity. 11: 3

A kind-hearted woman gains respect but ruthless men gain only wealth. 11: 16

One man gives freely, yet gains even more; another withholds unduly, but comes to poverty 11: 24

A generous man will prosper; he who refreshes others will himself be refreshed. 11:25

He who seeks good finds goodwill, but evil comes to him who searches for it. 11: 27

Whoever loves discipline loves knowledge, but he who hates corrections is stupid12: 1

All hard work brings profit, but mere talk leads only to poverty. 14: 23

A happy heart makes the face cheerful, but heartache crushes the spirit. 15:13

Better a meal of vegetables where there is love, than a fattened calf with hatred. 15: 17

Pleasant words are a honey-comb, sweet to the soul and healing to the bones. 16:24

He who covers over an offence promotes love, but whoever repeats the matter separates close friends. 17: 9

He who answers before listening, that is his folly and his shame. 18: 13

Casting the lot settles disputes and keeps strong opponents apart. 18:18

A man's wisdom gives him patience; it is to his glory to overlook an offence. 19: 11

Listen to advice and accept instruction, and in the end you will be wise. 19: 20

Many a man claims to have unfailing love, but a faithful man, who can find? 20: 6

Gold there is and rubies in abundance, but lips that speak knowledge are a rare jewel. 20: 15

Better to live on a corner of the roof than share a house with a quarrelsome wife.21: 9

A good man is more desirable than riches; to be esteemed is better than silver or gold. 22: 1

Do not make friends with a hot tempered man, do not associate with one easily angered, or you may learn his ways and get ensnared. 22: 24 -25

Do not wear yourself out to get rich, have the wisdom to show restraint. 23: 4

By wisdom a house is built, and through understanding it is established, through knowledge its rooms are filled with rare and beautiful treasures. 24: 3

Do not answer a fool according to his folly, or you will be like him yourself. 26: 4

Speak up for those who cannot speak for themselves, for the rights of all who are destitute; speak up and judge fairly; defend the rights of the poor and needy. 31: 8

Associations...

20 Proverbs

It is amazing that so many sayings over two thousand years old still are highly relevant. It is equally puzzling that so many obviously wise and useful proverbs are still ignored and disregarded. It is not only a matter of learning about the right things and conduct, this learning needs to be continuously reinforced and brought to attention. As generations come and go the accumulated wisdom needs to be passed across to the young, ideally refined and improved upon by each new generation. Is this happening? Are we getting wiser, more loving, and more compassionate? I would like to think so, but progress is very precious and needs attention and nurturing. The risk of losing direction and going astray is ever present. Keeping to the path of love and understanding is not necessarily natural but is acquired through the spirit, the spirit of one-ness and unity. Although Proverbs is full of eternal wisdom, I comment on but a few paragraphs below.

Most parents realize that learning and education are the best gifts they can give to their offspring. And it is not so much a matter of absorbing skills, which is also important, but far beyond the importance of skills, is the acquisition of character and harmony of the soul. This is wisdom to understand and appreciate the richness of life and not get caught up in trivial pursuits or pride. Once blessed with an understanding of wisdom, you can never move back, never lose out, because whatever you have gained remains, and what misfortune might strike you is only providing contrast to the deeper blessings enjoyed, like the knots between the pearls of a beautiful necklace. This gold on the inside will always be more valuable than any worldly glitter. It helps you chose right over wrong and refrain from entertaining any ideas of gain at the expense of others. "Though it cost you all you have, get understanding."

Without a kind heart, all you do loses its meaning and beauty. When you set the purpose of your industry in the perspective of an expression of your care for your fellow man, and test all ideas and actions against its alignment with such higher purpose, then you know that you cannot go wrong. This doesn't mean your business will succeed in economic terms but it makes any success more sustainable and credible, reducing the risk of falling into your own trap. Even if your capital is gone you will retain your good will.

Capital is but money whereas good will is your good ideas, networks and friendships and the accumulated gratitude of all you have helped. The one, capital, can be replaced, the other, goodwill, nigh impossible to replace. Keeping your reputation intact allows you to rise again - loosing it can make you an outcast. If all you do is trying to gain advantage at my expense, why should I care, or not rejoice, if you go out of business. 'She who is kind hearted and seeks good finds goodwill. A noble character is worth more than rubies.'

All of us are certainly more capable than one of us. The practice in most schools to rank people in percentiles trains the mind to focus on being better than your friends and class- mates. We must be more careful with this practice because once out of school an attitude of trying to out maneuver and outdo your colleagues is devastating for the cohesion and team play necessary for any successful campaign.

Key is not to establish who is best, making all but one feel like losers, but to establish what the relative strengths are of each and every one so as to maximize the effect of the joint effort. Cicero tells us that it is foolishness in extreme to rank the value of sight and hearing, hands and feet - each deserve admiration and it is the utility of the combination that enables a wholesome fully fledged life. Thinking that you have nothing to learn from others surely can only lead downhill to conceit, arrogance and stagnation. Whatever we do is ultimately for the consumption of people and if we feel contempt for the ultimate customer we are heading for disaster. Bertrand Russell reminds us that it is unlikely that others will think better of you than you think of them. 'A wise man listens to advice.'

Imagining unlimited plenty and gluttony may create a soothing dream for a hungry heart, but getting there can only prove an illusion - like the rainbow's end. It is the meaningful and loving interaction between people that provide the ultimate high and satisfaction. The beauty of it is that this is there for all to taste, almost regardless of wealth and means.

It is very easy to say things in haste that may hurt intentionally or unintentionally. Quite often the purpose isn't half as vicious as perceived by the offended party and picking it up and arguing it only confers unwarranted status on the person or the matter. Leave it by the wayside and any onlooker or audience will be able to see it for what it is. Pick it up and you are on a slippery slope that can well lead to widespread contempt and disaster. Is it bigger than you, or are you bigger than it? 'A man's wisdom gives him patience; it is to his glory to overlook an offence.'

True love and personal spirituality is about substance and not about form. There is no merit in showing off; merit lies in always trying to act lovingly without reproach and there is tremendous reward in even the smallest contribution to the generation of beauty and generosity. 'To do what is right and just is better than sacrifice. Speak up for those who cannot speak for themselves, defend the rights of the poor and needy.'

IV Ecclesiastes through Ezekiel with Associations

21. Ecclesiastes

The main theme of the Ecclesiastes is that everything is meaningless - pleasure, wisdom, folly and toil - but there are many beautiful and poetic parts.

What does a man gain from all his labor at which he toils under the sun? Generations come and generations go, but the earth remains the same forever. The sun rises and the sun sets, and hurries back to where it rises, the wind blows to the south and turns to the north; round and round it goes, ever returning to its course. 1: 3 - 6

I saw that wisdom is better than folly, just as light is better than darkness. The wise man has eyes in his head but the fool walks in the darkness. 1: 13 - 14

There is a time for everything and a season for all activity under heaven:

a time to be born and a time to die,
a time to plant and a time to uproot,
a time to kill and a time to heal,
a time to tear down and a time to build,
a time to weep and a time to laugh,
a time to mourn and a time to dance,
a time to scatter stones and a time to gather them,
a time to embrace and a time to refrain,
a time to search and a time to give up,
a time to keep and a time to throw away,
a time to tear and a time to mend,
a time to be silent and a time to speak,
a time to love and a time to hate,
a time for war and a time for peace. 1: 3 - 8

There is nothing better for a man than to enjoy his work, because this is his lot. 3: 22

If one falls down, his friend can help him up. But pity the man who falls and has no one to help him up! If two lie down together, they will keep warm. But how can one keep warm alone? Though one may be overpowered, two can defend themselves. A cord of three strands is not quickly broken. 4:10 - 12

It is better not to make a vow than to make a vow and not fulfill it. 5: 4

Whoever loves money, never has money enough; whoever loves wealth is never satisfied with his income. 5: 10

The sleep of a laborer is sweet, whether he eats little or much, but the abundance of a rich man permits him no sleep. 5: 12

Naked a man comes from his mother's womb and as he comes, so he departs. 5: 15

A good name is better than fine perfume. 7: 1

The end of a matter is better than its beginning, and patience is better than pride. Do not be quickly provoked in your spirit, for anger resides in the lap of fools. 7: 8 - 9

When times are good be happy; but when times are bad consider: God has made the one as well as the other. Therefore, a man cannot discover anything about his future. 7: 14

Do not be over-righteous, neither be over-wise - why destroy yourself? Avoid all extremes. 7: 16 - 18

Wisdom brightens a man's face and changes its hard appearance. 8: 1

I commend the enjoyment of life, because nothing is better for a man under the sun than to eat and drink and be glad. 8: 15

Anyone who is among the living has hope - even a live dog is better off than a dead lion. 9: 4

Go, eat your food with gladness, and drink your wine with a joyful heart, for it is now that God favors what you do. 9: 7

The quiet words of the wise are more to be heeded than the shouts of a ruler of fools. Wisdom is better than weapons of war. 9: 17 - 18

However many years a man may live, let him enjoy them all. Be happy, young man, while you are young, and let your heart give you joy in the days of your youth. Follow the ways of your heart and whatever your eyes see, but know that for all these things God will bring you to judgment. Banish the troubles of your heart and cast off the troubles of your body. 11: 9-10

Associations...

21 Ecclesiastes

Our children are everything! But aren't we also children, and weren't our parents and grand parents? Just as our children may well become parents and grandparents. Hopes and aspirations, a desire to achieve and improve, yes! Extinguishing yourself in a blind ambition to look around the corner, no! Behind every corner, there is a new corner. Thus it is imperative that in your search for new vision, you accept and enjoy the process. Because forever continuing process is all there is. The journey leads nowhere. The journey is it. See, smell, touch, taste, learn and love. Be happy and do good while you live - eat, drink and find satisfaction in your toil - this is the gift of God.

Worry is a human trait and often taken advantage of by religious zealots and also in sales and marketing. Through the industrialized world one of these worries is that people live longer and have fewer children. But wait a minute! Isn't that exactly what we all said we were striving for? A long happy high quality life for all; and to have children in such number as to allow development, health, love and attention for each and every one, and consistent with a sustainable usage of the world's resources.

Although world population has grown enormously in the last one hundred years, per capita income has grown ten times as fast. Low population growth is not a problem. Look to immigration and enjoy the higher quality of life. Long life is not a problem. It is a blessing. With the progress and gains in medicine, an eighty year old lives more comfortably today than a sixty five year old did fifty years ago. And the odds are nine to one that it is only going to get better.

There won't be enough jobs in future and there won't be enough people working to provide for the elderly. When you think about these two quite common concerns it is obvious that they off-set each other. They cancel each other out. Don't worry so much.

Many people tell us to save more. It all boils down to a balance. The challenges are not greater than in the past, they are smaller as efficiency gains mean that fewer and fewer people can achieve more and more. Some err on frivolity. Some err on being overcautious and over zealous. On balance there are more and more resources available both on an absolute and relative basis and thus we should worry less and not more.

So is there nothing to worry about? Worry has a negative connotation and there is no reason to be negative about the present or the future. There are many challenges - but challenges are the essence of life. No challenge - no life! We need to vigorously promote love and compassion. But that is not done through fear or worries, but by tolerance, wisdom and education, promoting cross border networks and friendships. And we owe it to ourselves to enjoy it and keep our spirits high in the process, to count our blessings. This creates enthusiasm, which helps progress towards a better order of things. It is happening. The world is getting better.

However many years a man may live, let him enjoy them all.

22. Song of Solomon

See! The winter is past; the rains are over and gone.
Flowers appear on the earth; the season of singing has come,
the cooing of doves is heard in our land.
The fig tree forms its early fruit; the blossoming vines spread their
fragrance.
Arise, come my darling, my beautiful one, come with me. 2: 11 - 13

E at, O friends, and drink; drink your fill, O lovers. 5: 1

How beautiful your sandaled feet, O prince's daughter!
Your graceful legs are like jewels, the work of a craftsman's hands.
Your navel is a rounded goblet that never lacks blended wine.
Your waist is a mound of wheat encircled by lilies.
Your breasts are like two fawns, twins of a gazelle.
Your neck is like an ivory tower.
Your eyes are the pools of Heshbon by the gate of bath Rabbim
Your nose is like the tower of Lebanon looking towards Damascus.
Your head crowns you like Mount Carmel
Your hair is like royal tapestry; the king is held captive by its tresses.
How beautiful you are and how pleasing!
O love with your delights!
Your stature is like that of the palm, and your breasts like clusters of
fruit.
I said, "I will climb the palm tree; I will take hold of its fruit.
May your breasts be like the clusters of the vine,
the fragrances of your breath like apples,
and your mouth like the best wine. 7: 1 – 9

Associations...

22 Song of Solomon

Driving to work in Tokyo I have been listening to the same CD with singing by Billie Holiday for a while and one tune has firmly etched itself into my mind. The combination of her singing, the delightful light jazz music and the loveliness of the lyrics kick me into a superb mood in the morning, ready to love everything and everyone. As I have been singing it daily and it only contains six lines I will share it with you here.

Just like a little old fashion music box with just one tune to play,
my heart keeps singing I love you twenty four hours a day.
Like a little old fashion music box might skip a note or two
My heart keeps missing a heartbeat singing a song about you
And although we know the song is old
It is still the sweetest story ever told.
Just like a little old fashion music box with just one tune to play,
my heart keeps singing I love you twenty four hours a day

There must be millions of these written over decades capturing the most exhilarating and beautiful of sensations that come to us in a lifetime. To be in a warm and close romantic relationship where the sensations of giving and receiving are inextricably intertwined has to contain some of the finest moments in anyone's life. And it is not as if this is available only to the lucky winner, the one in a million like in most other lotteries. In the lottery of life the most precious of prizes is out there waiting for all - love can come, not only to anyone, but in fact to everyone. The best things in life are free.

So does this happen only once in a lifetime? By definition a premier can only happen once. Det sker blott en gång? Es gibt nur einmal! If there is a second time it cannot quite contain the same sensation of entering new divine territory of unprecedented elevation. This is not necessarily sad. Perhaps one can get a bit melancholy about it. And we can and should all appreciate what has been given us and not be sad over what is not. The very nature of the ultimate and most unique beauty is that it is passing. That is what makes it so precious and beautiful. And a rich life goes on to offer many more sensations and firsts.

Love may change her dress but she is the best and finest partner to cling to throughout life. Dance with her every day. Keep her in your dreams.

I hesitate to even try to comment on the lines from Song of Songs above. It speaks for itself and like love is best experienced personally. Clothing it in more words may well reduce rather than enhance her beauty. But in a lovely way it does say yes to both body and soul in a sincere uninhibited flow of prose. Surely we were given both, to cherish, experience and enjoy gratuitously. Love is life.

23. Isaiah

S top doing wrong, learn to do right! Seek justice and encourage the oppressed. Defend the case of the fatherless, plead the case of the widow. 1: 17

He will judge between the nations and will settle disputes for many peoples. They will beat their swords into ploughshares and their spears into pruning hooks. Nation will not take up sword against nation, nor will they train for war any more. 2: 4

The arrogance of man will be brought low and the pride of men humbled. 2: 17

Woe to those who make unjust laws, to those who issue oppressive decrees, to deprive the poor of their rights, and withhold justice from the oppressed of my people. 10: 1 - 2

The oppressor will come to an end and destruction will cease; the aggressor will vanish from the land. In love a throne will be established; in faithfulness a man will sit on it. 16: 4 - 5

Take up a harp, walk through the city, O prostitute forgotten; play the harp well, sing many a song, so that you will be remembered. 23:16

He who walks righteously and speaks what is right, who rejects gain from extortion and keeps his hands from accepting bribes, who stops his ears against plots of murder and shuts his eyes against contempt and evil - this is the man who will dwell on the heights whose refuge will be the mountain fortress, his bread will be supplied, and water will not fail him. 33: 15 - 16

You have seen many things, but you have paid no attention; your ears are open, but you hear nothing. 42: 20

Shout for joy, O heavens; rejoice O earth; burst into song, O mountains. 49: 13

Awake, awake, cloth yourself with strength. 51: 9

How beautiful on the mountain are the feet of those who bring good news; who proclaim peace, who bring good tidings. 52: 7

If you do away with the yoke of oppression, with the pointing finger and malicious talk, and if you spend yourselves on behalf of the hungry and satisfy the needs of the oppressed, then your light will rise in the darkness, and your night will become like noonday. The LORD will guide you always; he will satisfy your needs in a sun- scorched land and will strengthen your frame. You will be like a well-watered garden like a spring whose waters never fail. 58: 9 - 11

I will make peace your governor and righteousness your ruler. No longer will violence be heard in your land, nor ruin or destruction within your borders. 60: 18

Your sun will never set again, and your moon will wane no more. 60: 20

I love justice; I hate robbery and iniquity. 61: 8

They will build houses and dwell in them; they will plant vineyards and eat their fruit. No longer will they build houses and others live in them, or plant and others eat. 65: 21 – 22

Associations...

23 Isaiah

Walk through the City, play the harp well, sing many a song. How beautiful on the mountain are the feet of those who bring good news, who proclaim peace, who bring good tidings. Be like a well-watered garden, like a spring whose water never fails.

Awake, awake, cloth yourself with strength. Make peace your governor and righteousness your ruler. Your sun will never set again, and your moon will wane no more. Love justice. Hate robbery and iniquity.

Both Plato and Confucius saw music as a department of Ethics. And it is almost impossible not to get a sense of love and compassion when touched by fine music. More music at work, more music at school, more music! The arts help us put other strivings and ambitions in perspective. Any asset, any relationship, any experience is only valuable to the extent that it makes us open our eyes and progress towards more and better friendships and a happier more fulfilled life. Song and dance and amateur sports serve the same purpose. If it is sports it has to be amateur, because as soon as we play for economic gain, the balance and relief from the struggle for survival is lost.

The line about 'prostitute forgotten' 23:16 has a very beautiful and eternal ring to it. I feel that we should not condemn too harshly any human behavior (other than physical or mental violence) knowing that no one is flawless. The much too common hypocrisy, including the religious kind, is more dangerous and detestable. And it often disguises itself in a way not available to prostitution and petty crime. Hypocrisy often leads to condemnation of others with much smaller flaws than the hypocrite. False labeling is nothing short of fraud. It is a catalyst for bigotry and unhappiness. We all do all sorts of things for money, most of the time within the rules of ethics and good values, but the person is not born who doesn't digress. To err is human. Forgiveness is divine. The best correction is compassion and tolerance and creating opportunities and incentives through information and education. Be transparent - say what you think. People should be able to pursue happiness by ways sought out in a climate of free choice rather than by compulsion for lack of alternatives.

The frustrations of life are more or less constant. Ambiguities, rivalry, lack of confidence. If you try your best to be like a never ending well of fresh water you will reduce unfriendliness and fear. Clothe yourself with strength. When we solve one problem we will face a new one. This is just the nature of things. In our work life we are often asked to do the impossible, i.e. double your revenue, halve your cost. Every year! This is to be seen as direction and trends rather than absolute requirements. All you can do is to understand and agree with the strategy - if you don't agree you should argue and (in extreme cases) possibly opt out, depending on the severity of the divergence of opinion - and then work towards the goal.

Don't worry about numerical targets. Instead ensure that there is no infighting, that the best possible spirit is achieved, that there is support and care for all team members (as well as customers, non-customers and suppliers), and that superior effort is applied in pursuing the goals. This is a recipe for happiness. Moreover, this approach always leads to results. Whether this is 80 % of plan or 120 % of plan is less relevant, the key is that the right soil will produce the best crop under the circumstances. Effort, trust and team spirit will put you in the best quartile of performers. And it is the relative performance, which reflects the quality of your team and leads to sustainable long-term achievement. We must be positive. Where there is effort, there is always something to rejoice over. Bring it out, let it shine and provide a stimuli and a star for future direction.

There are three key ingredients in successful business; people, capital and reputation. People are paramount, capital is important but reputation is absolutely crucial. Love justice. Hate robbery and iniquity. By defining and emphasizing how our business serves humanity we have the potential to lever unlimited support from everywhere. Being unclear or vague in these respects severely reduces inherent potential.

24. Jeremiah

An account of how Jerusalem - as prophesied by Jeremiah - was delivered in the hands of Nebuchadnezzar and the Babylonians. Jerusalem burnt and destroyed and the Israelis killed or scattered. The lowest allowed to stay, and cultivate the land.

I will give you shepherds after my own heart, who will lead you with knowledge and understanding. 3: 15

How gladly would I treat you like sons and give you a desirable land, the most beautiful inheritance of any nation. 3: 19

Go up and down the streets of Jerusalem, look around you and consider, search through her squares. If you can find but one person who deals honestly and seeks the truth, I will forgive this city. 5: 1

From the least to the greatest, all are greedy for gain; prophets and priests alike, all practice deceit. 6: 13

"Who will have pity on you, O Jerusalem? Who will mourn for you? Who will stop to ask how you are? You have rejected me," declares the LORD. "You keep on backsliding. So I will lay hands on you and destroy you; I can no longer show compassion." 15: 5 - 6

He will be like a tree planted by the water that sends its roots out by the stream. It does not fear when heat comes; its leaves are always green. It has no worries in a year of drought and never fails to bear fruit. 17: 8

He did what was right and just, so all went well with him. He defended the cause of the poor and needy, and so all went well. 22:16

I have loved you with an everlasting love; I have drawn you with loving kindness. I will build you up again, and you will be rebuilt, O virgin Israel. Again you will take up your tambourines and go out to dance with the joyful. Again you will plant vineyards on the hills of Samaria; the farmers will plant them and enjoy their fruit. 31: 3 - 5

They will be like a well-watered garden and they will sorrow no more. The maidens will dance and be glad, young men and old as well. I will turn their mourning into gladness;

I will give them comfort and joy instead of sorrow. 31: 12 - 13
Every man is senseless without knowledge. 51: 17

Associations...

24 Jeremiah

The Shinkansen (bullet train) brought me to Kyoto via Yokohama and Nagoya so swiftly and easily. Everything spotless and on the dot, friendly and helpful people, kindly bridging the language gap, making travel like a lovely dance. Bilateral two-day discussions between Japanese and Kiwis (New Zealanders) on improved co-operation in a setting of brightly autumn-colored trees, water and birds. One hundred people basically from two nations in a large room and the messages were loud and clear, particularly the unspoken, implicit messages; 'Let's try harder to do more for each other for trade, education, enjoyment and quality of life.'

Not one person in the room uncommitted to improving the quality of the dance, the hosts being the more humble. Being big and (basically) financially strong and Japanese, the hosts were cautious to not let the unbalance of importance and strength on the world stage hamper the constructive sense of two peoples equally entitled to seek success in the world. And if all are focused on shared success, there is potential not only for great improvement but something finer and higher than that, i.e. universal fellowship and brotherhood. As usual there were too few sisters and young people around, but there were some and the trend is clear and inevitable towards more balance and diversity. Sometimes it seems that women can see clearer that avenues harming the fauna and the flora, drinking water and the air we breathe, obviously are unsustainable and really inexcusable. Thereby women can help to put (male dominated) business endeavors in perspective and ensure that goals are consistent with the interest of society.

Not one harsh word spoken from any of many participants. Does this make the conference less effective? I don't think so - if all are positive and constructive, earnestly emphasizing affection and mutual benefit, nothing but good can come of it. It needs to be complemented with the resolve to implement and see progress through, to improve conditions, not only for the present parties, but for the benefit of third parties as well. World Citizenship requires an all-inclusive view of advancement, albeit that a step-by- step approach often is the only way forward.

The key speaker from Kyoto emphasized that the best most constructive progress comes from small-scale ventures, mixing art and sciences. Business without music is like production without marketing and consumption. I am not sure he said exactly that but that is how I heard him. If we but look and listen intently enough, sooner or later we find beautiful people and hear the music.

Committing to the just and fruitful concern and interaction with others is committing to love and life. As I am writing this down my radio plays a tune from the nineteen forties and this lovely line unfolds: 'We were so happy, the room was singing love songs and dancing up and down.' Imbued with thoughts of how to benefit others has the potential to send us onto formidable highs. One of the Japanese delegates approached several of the guest participants and asked; please tell me how you see the current challenges for Japan - what can we do to get through the current difficulties and end ten years of economic stagnation?

Anyone including myself who was asked I am sure felt quite humbled by the question, as it would be presumptuous to make out that we outsiders knew exactly what to do. Any thorough change must be a change of soul and direction that can only happen if embraced from within. I suggested that perhaps there need to be more focus on play and happiness. As president Roosevelt said in the nineteen thirties: 'the only thing we have to fear is fear itself.' View the world a bit more playfully and some of the knots in the stomachs that take vitality and pleasure out of life may dissipate and go away. ' It ain't that bad.' Let's find new ways to add value to others and ourselves.

Returning from the Japan - New Zealand conference on a clear day I got a fine view of the divine Fuji-san and fed my soul some eternal thinking from a book by Tolstoy. I was looking forward to the evening's concert at Tokyo 'Suntory Hall' with The Stuttgart Radio Orchestra playing music by the English composer Elgar for a couple of Swedes as well as three thousand other locals and foreigners. Japan, New Zealand, Russia, Germany, Great Britain, Sweden in one day. And the next day we found ourselves on a full day autumn-colors nature trip, arranged by a group of Japanese language teachers, with Japanese, Americans, English, Norwegians, Dutch and Italians, singing, walking, watching, BBQing, making it obvious that the world is coming together.

The British chancellor, Gordon Brown said in a speech in New York this week: 'Not only do we have inescapable obligations beyond our front doors and garden gates, responsibilities beyond the city hall and duties beyond our national boundaries, but this generation has it in our power - if it so chooses - to abolish all forms of human poverty.' The chancellor said that the forces of globalization and free trade now had to be harnessed to bring prosperity to the developing world.

The key messages from Jeremiah seem to provide good food for thought harmonizing in some ways with different parts of the last days' experiences: Do what is right and just and defended the cause of the poor and needy. Be like a well-watered garden and sorrow no more. Dance and be glad, maidens, young men and old. Turn mourning into gladness; Seek comfort and joy instead of sorrow. Take up your tambourines and go out to dance with the joyful. Plant vineyards and enjoy their fruit. Lead with knowledge and understanding. Every man is senseless without knowledge.

25. Lamentations

S hort but very poetic reflections on the state of Jerusalem after the devastation.

How deserted lies the city, once so full of people! How like a widow is she who once was great among the nations! She who was queen among the provinces has now become a slave. Bitterly she weeps at night, tears are upon her cheeks. Among all her lovers there is none to comfort her. All her friends have betrayed her; they have become her enemies. 1: 1 - 2

My eyes fail from weeping. I am in torment within. My heart is poured on the ground because my people are destroyed, because children and infants faint in the streets of the city. They say to their mothers, where is bread and wine - as they faint like wounded men in the streets of the city, as their life ebb away in their mothers arms. 2:11-12

Is this the city that was called the perfection of beauty, the joy of the whole earth? 2: 15

Associations...

25 Lamentations

Is there anything positive with destruction and suffering and the tearing down of walls and houses? Even if something rises out of the ashes, why is the scorching fire necessary? Questions are easy to ask, answers are often difficult to find. From Confucius we learn: "To understand Destiny is to know that certain things come under the sway of Destiny and that it is futile to pursue them." So the answer is that there is no obvious answer for us to see. However, if we cling on to virtue and love and tolerance with all our might, and build our society on respect, law and justice, we may be able to reduce and minimize evil and indiscriminate and unspeakable pain.

A central role of religion and the bible seems to me to be to organize a better society where a good, peaceful and happy life is possible and extended to ever more people. In that respect there seems to have been considerable success. The average per capita income of today's six billion people is infinitely higher than individual income ever was in the history of mankind. This does not mean that there is no suffering or hate, that there is no murder and devastation. When more and more are trying to create better living conditions for all, the inevitable occasional misfortunes, crimes and atrocities have to be borne with equanimity. And good forces from all over the world, regardless of religious denomination, must and will continue to improve conditions for mankind. We should rejoice that there is a markedly positive trend in human living conditions and treatment of each other. And at the same time never cease to work on improvements.

Whatever happens, our resolve to progress and improve must stand fast. Despair will get us nowhere and is therefore unproductive and wrong. The most important form of leadership, leading mankind forward to a more harmonious coexistence, requires vision, enthusiasm, optimism and energy by people, who are all-inclusive in their love for humanity. As soon as anyone is excluded from the journey, there is division and dissatisfaction that may fester and ultimately become lethal. This is a fine equation, which is essentially unstable, such that positive correction and adjustment is forever necessary. And the quality, character and stature by those entrusted to make these adjustments decide the degree of success.

With a rising level of human education and interconnectedness there is every reason to believe and hope that a better order is underway. However, we must not slacken. And we must forever and constantly remind ourselves of the virtues of tolerance, empathy and love which all provide essential lubricants for harmony and happiness.

The grim and sad fate of Jerusalem would have been replicated thousands of times in numerous places during the course of history.

Although similar tragedies still happen it is with less frequency. The most important responsibility of ours, and our children's, is to nurture and improve on this inherited trend. We all need to ensure we pass the test every day.

For Jerusalem! For mankind! For harmony! For love!

26. Ezekiel

E zekiel, the priest, prophesies the fall of Jerusalem and the scattering of Israel. It explains how grave breaches had been committed justifying the downfall. There is also an account of Tyre's downfall, and finally the beginning of the restoration of Jerusalem.

Do not be afraid, though briers and thorns are all around you and you live among scorpions. Do not be afraid of what they say or terrified by them, though they are a rebellious house. 2: 6

Take wheat and barley, beans and lentils, millet and spelt; put them in a storage jar and use them to make bread for yourself. 4: 9

Their silver and gold will not be able to save them. 7: 19

I bring down the tall tree and make the low tree grow tall. I dry up the green tree and make the dry tree flourish. 17: 24

He does not lend at usury and take excessive interest. He withholds his hand from doing wrong and judges fairly between man and man. 18: 8

The son will not share the guilt of the father. 18: 20

Rid yourself of all the offences you have committed, and get a new heart and a new spirit. 18: 31

The lowly will be exalted and the exalted will be brought low. 21: 26

Association...

26 Ezekiel

This is perhaps one of the less known books, painting a picture of decay and the way out of it. Recovery is something virtually all have to face in the course of a lifetime - being in a position we would rather not be in and have the wherewithal to devise a scheme to get out. The many descriptions of decay I have intentionally left out of this text and concentrated on the remedies and the way forward. We all have our own difficulties without delving too deeply into fictional others'. What we are hungry for is the way out - the way to correct our wrongs and cling to what is important.

With reference to the shocking events in New York and Washington DC the 11th September 2001, the Americans are saying we won't have our way of life threatened by some fanatics and madmen from remote countries. There is something rational and some justification for such reasoning. But there may also be something haughty and arrogant about it. To change and improve our ways is not the sign of resignation but a sign of strength and health. And whatever life we wish to live for ourselves, whichever way we seek to pursue happiness, our pursuit must also allow and not exclude others seeking their own ways. If our ways are intolerant and selfish, then we are in the wrong.

Throughout the history of mankind it has been incumbent on each individual and each generation to try to improve their lot, to try to give their off spring a better start than they got themselves. This is also true from taking up any kind of task or job - that we feel we have to improve on whatever we were asked to run and look after. Thus it is always wrong to assume that your adversary or anyone who seeks change is mad, but very healthy to ask yourself what you might do differently to improve your well being and avoid the predicament you may find yourself in. And if other people completely lack the means to improve themselves, the frustration of not being able to improve could well ignite hatred and unruly behavior.

Criminal acts must be persecuted, but, if you don't try to understand the reason for such acts, you may well disregard the real cause for it and fuel the fire rather than extinguish it. Has America gone astray? Perhaps the whole western world has to some extent with America leading the way. More and more people are worried about short-termism and lack of compassion and concern for the future of the world. With the modern communication techniques political leaders need to be so much wiser and more cautious than was the case historically. Anything said in American media is immediately available to the world. The temptation to appeal to American voters by suggesting they have a better right to enjoy life than other world citizens is naturally resented by others.

It really is passe even try to maximize the quality of life for your constituents, other than in harmony with seeking similar progress for all. It is both wrong and futile insofar as it directly or indirectly builds up resentment and hate by others and that cannot but deduct from the quality of life otherwise possible. With America so involved with world affairs it is a bit of an anomaly that only Americans get to decide on foreign policy and other issues. What are the chances for a president who has his main support in back-water America and with little experience of the world to understand and be acceptable to the rest of the world?

He who has the most munitions and capital has to be right? This is such an obviously flawed outlook so one wouldn't really have to try to disprove it. In fact most people tend to think the opposite - that the guy with all the muscles and money is more likely to be arrogant than fair. As people get better and better education, more needs to be put into communicating, explaining and positioning. And nothing but the truth communicated sincerely will do. People around the world nowadays are too smart and up to the play to be conned in the ways of the past.

In his book Utopia, Sir Thomas More says:

"There is no punishment so horrible that it can keep men from stealing, which have no other craft whereby to get their living. For great and horrible punishments be appointed for thieves, whereas much rather provision should have been made that there were some means whereby they might get their living, so that no man should be driven to this extreme necessity, first to steal, and then to die."

Says Thomas Paine in 'Rights of Man:' "The idea that you can govern by terror instead of reason is base and false. Man is not an enemy of man but through the false system of Government." We must accept that all human beings have equal right to pursue happiness and if one is severely disadvantaged in that pursuit through lack of nourishment or education the game is skewed and unfair and unhealthy tension is likely to build up.

The passage from the fourth chapter on baking bread reminds us that happiness is to toil for something worthwhile, followed by enjoyment - wine, song, dance shared among good friends - all concepts referred to frequently in the bible. Every day chores and effort must be mixed with reward and celebration in a brew of happiness. The things that stir our hearts remain the same over the millennia. Violence must be replaced by wisdom.

27. Daniel

Daniel, son of Judah, interpreted Nebudchadnezzar's dream and became his confidant. Daniel humbled both Nebudchadnezzar and his son and made them recognize the God of Israel. Daniel survives the den of the lion.

To the peoples, nations and men of every language, who live in the whole world: May you prosper greatly! 4: 1

Those who are wise will shine like the brightness of heavens, and those who lead many to righteousness, like the stars forever and ever. 12: 3

Associations...

27 Daniel

The score is kept. A majority of people across races and religions act on this basis. We feel that things are loop sided unless we do something positive from time to time, to at least compensate for our digressions. We have received the blessed life and our sense of reciprocity makes us want to demonstrate some generosity and appreciation. Does storing up positives allow you to digress and thus put you in credit? Neither life nor individuals are or should be as calculating as that. We don't need to seek out the negatives, the liabilities. They are there anyway and will be targets for our choices, bad choices, from time to time. But if we are aware that they are bad choices and if we feel a strong urge to compensate for deviations, we are human, we are OK. Without the bad option, how would we be able to identify the good option? Good means, more often than not, to seek out the goodness, to be a credit to yourself, your parents, your children, and to mankind.

Why is it that we are so focused that we may do all sorts of unsustainable and bad things to the environment and ourselves, only to compensate later by trying to do the opposite? Through shady practices many get rich only to later turn around and give the money back. Going fishing, only to put the fish back! Working sixty hours a week only to save money and be able to have a long or fancy vacation. Giving our kids away so we can work and provide better for them when we all know that the best things we can give them are time, life, love and experiences! But somehow this obvious truth gets pushed aside? Avoiding the extremes and introducing more balance must be beneficial for quality of life.

Building a family is a challenge. You marry a promise that most likely will not find its full deliverance. You are so excited with independence, setting up on your own, and perhaps intoxicated by love and sensuality, that you can't wait to see all these hopes and dreams fulfilled. For most, if not for all, the gap between the dreams and realizations will not be closed. Dreams act as carrots and incentives to move on and long for the next day, but the very nature of dreams and hope is that they don't usually come true. If they did, we might loose some of the most important and charming ingredients of life: dreams and hope.

Children personify dreams and hope. Often, perhaps even more often than not, they do deliver on improvement of mankind. They know more, they are more traveled and open-minded, they are less corruptible, and have less of fear and misery. But they will not be the perfect manifestations of generosity and goodness that we may hope them to be. Perfection is an eternal pursuit; nothing really important will ever be fully realized and achieved. The beauty of life through the generations is that there is always something to get passionate about, something to improve and something to strive towards. There always will be.

Key to personal happiness is to ensure that a majority of our thoughts and actions bring us forward in a positive direction. When we have set backs because of bad decisions, ill thoughts or poor execution or bad luck or a combination we need to be a bit generous to ourselves.

We must realize that the person that doesn't digress isn't human. We need to identify where we went wrong or what went wrong, pick up the pieces and start again. The gift of life is that every day gives us a new brilliant and unique chance to do a little bit better, to make progress. Love is the spice that does it. The inevitable and eternal gap between perfection and reality is bridged by love.

28. Hosea

Hosea told to go and take an adulterous wife and try to reform her.

There is no faithfulness, no love, no acknowledgement of God in the land. There is only cursing, lying and murder, stealing and adultery; they break all bounds and bloodshed follows bloodshed. Because of this the land mourns, and all who live in it waste away; the beasts of the field and the birds of the air and the fish of the sea are dying. 4: 1 - 3

I will heal their waywardness and love them freely, for my anger has turned away from them. I will be like the dew to Israel; he will blossom like a lily. Like a cedar of Lebanon he will send down his roots; his young shoots will grow. His splendor will be like an olive tree, his fragrance like a cedar of Lebanon. Men will dwell in his shade. He will flourish like the corn. He will blossom like a vine, and his fame will be like the wine from Lebanon. 14: 4 – 7

Associations...

28 Hosea

'The land mourns, and all who live in it waste away; the beasts of the field and the birds of the air and the fish of the sea are dying.' This could well be a current headline in any newspaper from around the world. Well, is it true or is it exaggerated?

Lee Kuan Yew says in his book 'From Third World to First' that 'progress and prosperity are not the natural order of things. They depend on ceaseless effort and attention.' Things constantly threaten to go off the rails unless positive action is taken to support improvement for mankind and discourage decay and extortion. This is equally true for the biggest global questions as for the smallest task at hand. With so many people in the world today the challenges and threats are greater than ever but this is mirrored by larger than ever opportunities to create sustainable harmony and improved quality of life for all.

It is up to our politicians. It is up to the voters. It is up to our teachers. It is up to Industry leaders. It is up to religious gurus. It is up to all parents. It is up to all children. It is up to you. It is up to me. It is a bit like a tug of war where we are saved if the side pulling towards fairness and understanding, tolerance and love, care and concern for the future pulls harder. Quality of character must be lifted up as a key priority and selection criteria in both Government and Industry. Strengthening values must take precedence over acquisition of skills - the former must be in check of the other. Not paying heed to ethics and environmental concerns - which broadly are the same - is a recipe for disaster. If an ambition to 'do good' is important, even more important is that we feel good. If we don't look happy, if our road is not strewn with flowers, song and dance, laughter and witticism, what credibility is there to our preaching of a better way? Increased happiness is the validity test.

Paul Hawken says in his book 'The Ecology of Commerce' that "business people must either dedicate themselves to transforming commerce to a restorative undertaking, or march society to the undertaker." "The promise of business is to increase the general well being of humankind through service, a creative invention and ethical philosophy." The hope must be that more and more people will see the light trying to build something better for the many without sacrificing individual rights. To nurture and protect the divine flame lit in every human at birth.

We all originally come from the earth. She must be respected and cherished and given loving care. Agriculture and farmers have out of proportion political influence in all countries for a reason. They are toiling with that which was our origin and that which is an integral necessary part of our future. In the book 'Cato and Varro on Agriculture' written in the second and first centuries B.C. the authors point out: "Remember that a farm is like a man - however great the income, if there is extravagance but little is left. See that the cattle always have good clear water to drink in the summer time; it is important for their health. Farmers antedate city people by an enormous amount of years - and no marvel since it was divine nature, which gave us the country, and man's skill that built the city."

Land and creatures must be treated with dignity and respect that we may be able to live in harmony among ourselves and that our children be given capital assets of at least equal value as when acquired by ourselves. The line I liked best in Lee Kuan Yew's book referred to above is: 'The best thing we ever did was planting millions of trees.' Seeing value where traditional measures and accounting see none. You only need to spend a few hours in Singapore and you know that he is right.

29. Joel

A call to repentance! Blessings for God's people.
I am sending you grain, new wine and oil, enough to satisfy you fully; never again will I make you the scorn of nations. 2: 19

Be not afraid, O wild animals, for the open pastures are becoming green. The trees are bearing their fruit; the fig tree and the vine yield their riches. 2: 22

Associations...

29 Joel

There is enough to go around. In the United Nations' headquarters in New York there is a poster that says that the annual spend on world military endeavors is about three times the total costs for correcting all known physical supply problems in the world including food, water and medicines. It is only a matter of co-operation, empathy, compassion and distribution to deal effectively with these problems. Although we are six billion people in the world today, a higher portion than ever enjoys freedom from material want. Even if we should hit the now predicted ten billion people before the population levels off, it can work, if we do it well and do it together. It is quite amazing that in two hundred years the world's population has multiplied tenfold and yet we have basically been able to cope.

And of course, the biblical stories of one people advancing and triumphing at the exclusion and expense of another, just isn't plausible anymore. Love and care, empathy and compassion don't lend themselves readily to any restrictions. By their very nature they are open-ended.

The conflicts need to be sorted out, because there is but one success formula for the world. This is where all come out as winners, where all share in the spoils of progress.

It is particularly painful to see the conflict in the Middle East, where three world religions meet, being unresolved, continuing disagreement and disarray. Religion is about being good, searching for virtue. To say that one religion is better than any other is in my view futile, and if three groups which through independent means are seeking the ultimate virtue and elevation, degenerate to killing each other in the pursuit of the highest good, we see how absurd it all becomes. They are not good at all; they are stuck in a cul-de-sac.

So how do we sort it out? Education and health including improvement of living conditions are paramount. Particularly the Palestinians need to be supported into proper housing and education so they can all have a share and stake in world progress. And immigration should be as open as possible, allowing all to settle where they want and from there participate in democratic processes. True religion doesn't rest on geography. It rests in soul and heart. The rest of the world need to lean on the antagonists and demonstrate to them that unethical and violent behavior will not be tolerated and will lead to exclusion from the world organizations and sharing in the benefits of aid and trade.

Clearly this isn't easy. The good news is that these ends are being targeted and pursued, but it takes time. Violence and murder can but lead to more violence and murder. Here is the challenge of love and forgiveness, and looking forward rather than backward. Do people really want their children to inherit this mess? The answer to this has to be no, other than for a minority of fanatics whom hatred have twisted beyond repair. Hatred always harms the hating more than the hated, and rightly so as the end of hate lies in their power to achieve.

The biggest industry in the world is tourism. All the countries in the Middle East, Lebanon, Syria, Jordan, Israel and Egypt as well as Iraq and Iran have formidable tourist attraction and potential, currently sadly at a very low utilization rate with enormous opportunity cost for businesses and families in the area. The many people, surely the majority, on both sides of the line, must find a way of asserting their desire for growth, peace and prosperity. As tension eases it should all be able to be open territory for living and visiting. That day will come in this century and it is in our hands to have it come sooner rather than later.

V Amos through Melachi with Associations

30. Amos

Judgment on Israel prophesying destruction, ending positively on what will follow.

Hate evil, love good; maintain justice in the courts. 5: 15

"The days are coming," declares the LORD, When the reaper will be overtaken by the ploughman and the planter by the one trading grapes. New wine will drip from the mountains and flow from all the hills. I will bring back my exiled people Israel; they will rebuild the ruined cities and live in them. They will plant vineyards and drink their wine; they will make gardens and eat their fruit. 9: 13 – 14

Associations...

30 Amos

Amos lived in the 8ᵗʰ century BC, the first Hebrew prophet to have a biblical book named after him. A prophet of doom, he accurately foretold the destruction of the northern kingdom of Israel. A native of Tekoa 12 miles south of Jerusalem he was a shepherd. He fiercely castigated corruption and social injustice. He believed that God compels social justice for all men, rich and poor alike - any breach against this creed inevitably will result in a penalty to pay. Self-indulgence, oppression of the poor and perversion of justice will be punished and righteousness rewarded. An eternally valid reminder to try to be the best we can be and not become too singular, overly focused on self, family, mammon, region, nation, religion, gender or race, but on all-inclusive love and compassion.

We are reminded of how the core issues stay the same and are forever relevant. We must have faith in God or good, and the purpose and beauty of good, to prevent eternal decay and disintegration. We must measure and align all our actions against the code of goodness and decency that better quality of life be achieved. What code of conduct and better for whom? I would suggest that the code is pretty universal - and that is perhaps how divinity reveals itself to me. That deep down we all know rather well what we can do and what we cannot in order that internal end external peace and harmony be attained and retained.

If this were true, why are there so many breaches of the obvious? Perhaps it is because all breaches are reported and make the news, whereas compliance and harmony as the norm doesn't draw much publicity and attention. The fact that we see so much violence and hatred reported in the media doesn't mean that we condone it. Having the privilege to live in Japan as my seventh country of abode makes it quite obvious that nine hundred and ninety nine acts out of a thousand are constructive acts, fully conversant with respect and love. But then there is the odd act ignoring all the values, which we believe in, and creating misery and misfortune and this is what makes the headlines.

In this context it may be opportune to express my distaste for violence as entertainment. This is really sick and no better than the Roman gladiator games. All sorts of things are censured around the world but the biggest breach and plague of them all - an endless stream of violence, torture and wounding and hurting people is considered acceptable entertainment for cinema or the family living room. I read somewhere that the average ten year old in America has seen in excess of five thousand entertainment murders. It is enough that one tenth of one percent of those exposed to this rubbish thinks that this is cool and acceptable behavior and take after these role models, for an endless amount of misery and fear to be created in our societies. I don't know how to wedge it out, but perhaps the first small step is to speak out against the practice and try to influence people not to support it.

31. Obadiah

The vision of Obadiah, judgment day is near.
You who say to yourselves, 'Who can bring me down to the ground'? Though you soar like the eagle and make your nest among the stars, from there I will bring you down. 1: 3 - 4

You should not look down on your brother in the day of his misfortune. 1: 12

As you have done, it will be done to you; your deeds will return upon your own head. 1: 15

Associations...

31 Obadiah

Two days before Christmas! Max my eldest son and his fiancé are to arrive at Narita this morning via Vienna but a fierce winter storm threw all flight schedules out of Stockholm and they ended up in Paris instead trying to catch another Paris -Tokyo flight, which they also missed. C'est la vie! We think we are going somewhere but circumstances change everything in a whim. But worse dislocations than Paris can easily be imagined. Two young people getting a bonus stay in this lovely city courtesy of the failing airline industry cannot be all bad. A line from Anatole France keeps knocking on my brains wanting desperately to get out: 'France is in Europe what a peach is in a basket of fruit; it is what is finest, sweetest, and most exquisite.' May they enjoy it. God willing, they will still be here the day before Christmas, i.e. 23rd December. For a Swede Christmas is the 24th December and to me that is of significance, because I used to feel special being born on Christmas, not the day before Christmas as my American friends would suggest.

The sun is slowly rising as I write this and I am listening to beautiful Christmas music - the absolute best of the best, which through the gains of technology, my son recorded on a CD yesterday. The old Greeks divided all human activity into Gynastica and Musica and since banking, my business, cannot really be said to be gymnastics, it must fall into the category of music. Like musicians, we must try to please the people and in a small way reach out and touch their souls. Banking? Can it really be done? I have no doubt it can be done in almost any business if we realize that whatever goods or services we are selling or promoting are only a means and not the end. The end is to try to have people feel good about themselves - to feel happy. If we can manage that, we have a relationship, the cornerstone for successful and sustainable business.

My wife has made it very Christmassy. A nice fir tree, almost like the ones we used to go out into the woods in Sweden and cut ourselves. She was unhappy that in spite of the high price for this tree in Tokyo it was more or less dead, but we all praised her for finding such a nice tree and in a few days it will have served its purpose well anyway. Our fifteen years old son decorated the tree - having been on the international circuit all his life, he loves tradition and relatives - both of which have been underrepresented in his life. You gain something, you loose something else - the condition of life - and if we are fortunate and positive we can count our blessings.

This particular Yoyogi Uehara Christmas tree had a story of its own. When my wife complained in the shop that the tree looked more dead than alive when decorated she immediately got 50% of the consideration back. She thought that quite generous and so did I. Three days later the kind male florist rang the bell on our apartment door to give all the money back. We found similar attitudes from our baker, dry cleaner and bottle shop – just no end to the care they would show to keep their customer happy. A very heart warming and inspirational experience!

It also smells Christmas - the scents from the kitchen promise quite a feast for a few days and stir emotions to recollect fragments from childhood Christmases. I have to find a few gifts for them all today -

usually something very symbolic and little from me as we are trying to provide everything needed on an ongoing basis anyway. Besides a few presents for family and friends, my wife has provided monetary gifts to a few people for whom it makes a big difference, like the daughter of our African maid. This somehow feels more meaningful than paying into a bottom less pit kind of charity, even if there are many admirable purposes among those as well. The value of money is only crystallized when spent or given away.

Generosity is the theme of the season. And even in business, generosity is the most palatable spice. If you are aiming to give people value for money, you may be aiming too low - we should try to make them feel they are getting more than the pay for, something that exceeds the value of the money consideration. As I talked to my mother last night, she said that the snow drifts were fast building up and at 82 and after a heart operation she should be very cautious about shoveling snow to clear her foot path. I suggested she call one of my old friends three houses away who I know would be delighted to help. There you have one of these situations where the effort of a helper is minute in comparison to the value created for the recipient. One unit of input is producing ten units of satisfaction. The concerns of someone wondering - will I be able to get out of my house today for my necessities - can be fully alleviated by ten minutes of healthy, quite pleasant and even fun work for a younger person. This is an example of a wonderful trade with only winners - epitomizing the beauty of life.

The value created is immeasurable, intangible, good will. Many businesses, politicians and countries would do well to try to increase their understanding of this concept. Focusing too much on numbers and financial returns may well take the beauty out of life and deplete the value of relationships. If people experience that 'I am onto something beautiful and good or I am working with the most self sacrificing, kindest and supportive people I have ever come across,' this feeling may well bring out extra energy and commitment that money cannot buy. Failing to stir the soul and spirit thus has a most significant opportunity cost.

If you ask people for quid pro quo, that is what you will get - if you are lucky! If you always try to stay in credit and give a little extra so will all those around you. Generosity once set in motion never stops.

As you have done it will be done to you. Amen.

32. Jonah

Jonah flees from the LORD out at sea and to quell a violent storm, he was thrown over board, swallowed by a big fish, and three days later thrown up on land. Jonah was angry for the compassion shown to a repenting city.

Those who cling to worthless idols, forfeit the grace that could be theirs. 2:8

What I have vowed, I will make good. 2:9

Let them give up their evil ways and their violence. Who knows? God may yet relent and with compassion turn from fierce anger so that we will not perish. 3: 8 - 9

I know that you are gracious and compassionate, slow to anger and abounding in love, relenting from sending calamity. 4:2

God provided a vine and made it grow up over Jonah to give shade for his head to ease his discomfort and Jonah was very happy about the vine. 4:6

Nineveh has more than a hundred and twenty thousand people who cannot tell their right hand from their left, and many cattle as well. Should I not be concerned about that great city? 4:11

Associations

32 Jonah

Life isn't always fair. You work hard, follow all the rules, and do all the right things. And yet someone ostensibly much less committed, much less righteous is doing equally well or better. Putting in so many hours a week and the next person on welfare seemingly does nothing and comes out almost the same.

But isn't this what forgiveness and compassion is for. If no one ever needed support, how would love express itself? We must recognize that even those less successful or those that have gone astray also have a soul, i.e. divinity hidden somewhere in their inner depths. Do we believe in the clinched fist or the extended open hand? Knowing that the flawless human being doesn't exist, should we focus on punishing flaws or encourage the exhibit of commendable social behavior? The one approach promotes love and cohesion, the other division and alienation.

But incentives, don't we need incentives? What we call civilization today is far too preoccupied with financial incentives, as if money was all that counted. This is an illusion and misconception. People well treated, exposed to love and generosity and having the benefit of a good education are very likely to be a credit to humanity without much financial incentive. Most people want to work and do a good job. The most gratifying aspect of any job is to make a difference and give and receive respect and appreciation. This goes an awfully long way and the perception that like a dumb and stubborn donkey, man won't move unless you keep the hey in his eyes is just a disgraceful underestimation of the miracle called homo sapiens. The French author Anatole France says it well in his book, Of Life and Letters IV, "Let us not criticize any more, let us only exhibit."

In debates, perhaps naturally, one outcome is argued over another, this is right and that is wrong. However in many cases such polarity is less than constructive. Life is more like playing the trombone. There are no fixed positions. Beauty and harmony must be pursued with care and experience and can only be learned after long and arduous training. Which is most important, food or spices? Without spices you can survive but not without food. But that doesn't make food more right than spice, the dichotomy is meaningless and futile. Can we contemplate a life without spices, colors, music and other things we may not strictly need? No, forget it! That is not life. Instead life is the exciting never-ending pursuit of the right blend, the most palatable brew. This will vary with time and place and from individual to individual. Each life is precious and unique and your music and brew may not be the choice of others. So be it, personal choice is one of the core wonders of life.

Overly focusing on punishment only means punishing ourselves, punishing mankind. Rather than punish let us all try to exhibit and role model. Love will always be greater driver than fear.

33. Micah

Judgment against Samaria and Jerusalem, Israel's guilt and punishment.

Woe to those who plan iniquity 2:1

He will judge between many peoples and will settle disputes for strong nations far and wide. They will beat their swords into ploughshares and their spears into pruning hooks. Nation will not take sword against nation, nor will they train for war any more. Every man will sit under his own vine and under his own fig tree and no one will make them afraid. 4: 3 - 4

Act justly and love mercy and walk humbly. 6: 8

You do not stay angry forever but delight to show mercy. You will again have compassion. 7: 18 – 19

Associations

33 Micah

When I decided to write a few lines as in this book I thought I would write to every odd book starting with Genesis and then, once finished with the odds, come back and restart with the evens, i.e. Exodus etc. This I did in order to increase the variety a bit. My thought pattern often gets into a particular territory and it takes new experiences or learning to expand and move onto new ground. I was hoping this might make it more palatable. At one stage I invited Linda, my wife, to do the evens and I think she gave Exodus a shot, but then decided that it was my baby and idea and that I should look after it and she get on with her own creations. Fair enough!

As I just passed Jonah on my way up the ladder it reminded me of an invitation I got in Singapore to attend a Baptist Congregation celebrating the 16 anniversary of a newly created church. The background to the invitation was a speech I gave on 'Happiness' to a Rotary Club in Singapore. One of my slides was 'What the Bible says about Happiness' and as I mentioned that I read the bible in its entirety to find these pearls, one of the participants asked for a copy of my 'Bible summary' and also invited me to his church. Not having participated in any church activity for many years, other than a few weddings, I thought it would be interesting for me as well as my son to go and see if it was for us. My son, then 14 years old, agreed to accompany me - my wife was away on a cultural trip to New Zealand. This is not an oxymoron - New Zealand has the most wonderful and impressive commitment to the arts, a commitment perhaps not well known overseas.

So on a March Sunday 2001 in 30 degrees C Singapore we got ready for church. We found the place, which was part of a school. Like many virgin congregations they didn't have their own church, but utilized an assembly hall at one of the local schools. I found the guy who invited me, and he most kindly introduced me to the pastor and many other attendees. To my and her surprise, one of my female staff was among the congregated and she came up and greeted me. She said she was surprised to see me there and I explained that I was invited for the anniversary celebration. Several people asked us which church we normally went to so we responded that we didn't belong to any special church.

We were the only 'westerners' so we did stand out a bit. I was impressed with how warm and friendly all were - no effort spared to try to make us at ease and feel welcome. The service started with a number of musical presentations by children of the congregation. Perhaps a bit amateurish, but absolutely lovely, to have several groups of young people come forward and perform their little pieces with delight. I thought that I could see how something like this once a week provides community and a booster for the soul.

Then the pastor got started. He spoke very clearly, confidently and audibly to all, a technique one would like to see espoused more in business as well. The Mass for the day was on Jonah and I delighted in knowing it in detail. People offered to lend us their bible, (as we didn't know we were supposed to bring one) but I could honestly say that I know Jonah. However, to my surprise he spent a long time talking about satan. Discretely I whispered to my son, that if there is one thing I don't believe in, it is satan. Since the universally and instinctively beautiful message of love is the essence of Jesus' teachings, how can we at the same time believe in satan? As far as I can recall nothing ever ascribed to Jesus' sayings or teachings ever included anything about satan. My spell check suggests I give satan a capital s which I refuse to do, so I get these red spots all over the screen. I can see how God and Good and Jesus justify capital letters, but satan, no, not in my book.

I felt the preacher was trying to terrorize the audience and scare them into submission. To me, this seems backwards and incompatible with the beautiful messages of love and compassion, forgiveness and generosity. I also reflect that 2,500 years ago - when some of the books may have been written - when speaking perhaps to brutes of limited education and sophistication some very clear divides and images may have been required to guide people to the right path. In the year 2001 with children and parents who are clean and neat, well educated and brought up in, and committed to, a civilized society, it is hard for me to see how it makes sense to fill a sermon with references to satan.

When later over the light meal the pastor asked me about my position, I explained that the love and compassion parts coming out of the book I endorse fully and unreservedly, whereas I have some problems with other parts reflecting violence and cruelty. He explained that it is one package and the only way to save yourself is to embrace the lot.

I just thanked him for the kind invitation and said how much I had appreciated it, the singing and the warm greetings by all the people. There was something fresh and young about such a new congregation of enthusiastic believers and I was an invited guest of theirs, so I was very cautious not to in any way challenge their beliefs or way of life. And I thought that my resolve and commitment to love and being the kindest most supportive and compassionate person that I can muster - fully aware there is and always will be room for improvement - will continue to be my leading star.

And as Micah reminds us: Act justly and love mercy and walk humbly.

34. Nahum

The city of Nineveh receives the punishment for its wickedness.
The Lord is slow to anger and great in power; the Lord will not leave the guilty unpunished 1: 3

Who can withstand his indignation? 1:6

Look there on the mountains, the feet of one who brings good news, who proclaims peace. Celebrate your festivals, o Judah, and fulfill your vows. 1: 15

Guard the fortress, watch the road, brace yourselves and marshal all your strengths. 2: 1

O king of Assyria, your shepherds slumber; your nobles lie down to rest. Your people are scattered on the mountains with no one to gather them. Nothing can heal your wound; your injury is fatal. Everyone who hears the news about you claps his hands at your fall, for who has not felt your endless cruelty? 3: 18 – 19

Associations...

34 Nahum

Gandhi said that anything conquered by violence can only be defended by violence. Violence breeds violence. Don't expect a rose to rise out of a planted thorn. It is quite horrifying to try to imagine how hoards of plunderers moved over the surface of the earth until modern times. The likelihood of meeting a violent death was historically very high in the whole world and perhaps especially so where your land lay at the crossroads for trade and migration. On the positive side at such crossroad your impressions and opportunity to learn from different cultures would have been high. But the risk that someone deviated from decency and peaceful trade rules must also have been very high.

Poverty and constant fear probably acted as promoters of religion and religious thought. The unification of souls and purpose through religion provided some spiritual relief to the constant threats of plunder, destruction, violence and physical abuse. Human morals suggest that he who steals, rapes and pillages is not ultimately going to get away with it. The ultimate reward in this world is to have people desire your well-being and do good to you in recognition for unselfish help, assistance and love. A tyrant and ill doer is forever denied such ultimate pleasure. Like the 'fastest-gun-in-the-West' always will have someone challenging him with a gun, the person who adopts violence as a means for achievement must always expect to live in fear of plots and assassinations.

A short quote from Gandhi may be in place: "Where there is only a choice between cowardice and violence, I would advice violence - but I believe that non-violence is infinitely superior to violence, forgiveness more manly than punishment. Forgiveness adorns a soldier. But abstinence is forgiveness only when there is power to punish. Strength does not come from physical capacity. It comes from an indomitable will."

This very much aligns with the basic messages of the New Testament. Regardless of how tangible the punishment is, to a vast majority of humanity, torment and regret comes from wrong-doing and seeking benefits by walking over corpses. New levels of education, new levels of affluence, allowing more and more people time to reflect, and increased communication, travel and migration should all contribute to making it clear and obvious that uncivilized and egotistical behavior will be revealed and not tolerated. It may be hard to believe sometimes but there is real hope for a better tomorrow. The world today is better than 30 years ago, better than 300 years ago and also better than 3000 years ago. In my view, the balance between love and fear, opportunity and threat, is improving. This does not mean that our list of things to do is getting shorter. It never will. Seeking further progress, we must all share in Gandhi's mission to extend compassion for all things living and put an end to oppression and violence.

35. Habakkuk

Habakkuk, the prophet, complains that too much violence and injustice is tolerated. The LORD assures him that revelation will come.

Woe to him who piles up stolen goods and makes himself wealthy by extortion! How long must this go on? Will not all your debtors suddenly arise? Will they not wake up and make you tremble? Then you will become their victim. Because you have plundered many nations, the people who are left will plunder you. 2: 6 -8

Woe to him who builds his realm by unjust gain to set his nest on high. 2: 9

He makes my feet like the feet of a deer; he enables me to go on the heights. 3: 19

For the director of music. On my stringed instruments.

Associations...

35 Habakkuk

These few lines scream to me that which I am trying to argue every day in the business world. There is no sustainable way other than the benevolent, caring and honest way. Yes, we can get away with less than that but certainly not in the long run. But slowing down and taking into consideration aspects other than growth and profits and shareholder wealth surely will make us less attractive to the investor community? This is a fallacy. It is like saving money by not having the necessary insurance or contingency plan or having more mast and sail than a rough day will allow you to get away with. It cannot end with anything but a crash. This is not good for investors. This is in fact putting shareholder value at great risk. This is no good at all.

It is sometimes pathetic the way business tries to influence people's action by incentive systems. With strong enough incentive systems to do wrong, many people will. The problem is when we get too clever with these things. Incentives in moderation can be reasonable stimuli but all too often - heads I win, tails you lose - situations are created. When we refine it and refine it and refine it we often go way beyond what actually makes sense. I think more women in business and more diversity has the potential to change and improve these aspects over the next century. Women often seem to be a bit closer to life and whatever is contrary to life and the laws of nature, is more likely to be exposed for what it is by women.

Don't manipulate people with incentive systems without having a thorough testing and understanding of the systems compatibility with ethics, caring and the creation of sustainable value. At the helm of this process must be a values-driven board or executive. Values are far too fundamental and important to be driven by some clever accountant. External pressures are much less effective than internal motivation.

A few years ago I was offered to be Managing Director for a large pension fund. When I was asked what my salary expectations were I said I was a bit uncertain since the job involved relocating to another country with its own wage structures. However, I mentioned an amount I thought would be reasonable and added that if things go really well, perhaps a bonus-recognition, as per some agreed formula, could be considered. I was immediately told that the salary was acceptable and the suggested bonus would be included in the salary, but no bonus would be considered. Here there was a view that anything that may threaten a commitment to values and ethics and to consider self before the stakeholders was undesirable. I thought the view very interesting and in some ways admirable. In the end I didn't take up the job but not for this reason.

Good leadership is about appealing to the divine core of people, lighting and nurturing the flame in every individual and perhaps even setting the soul ablaze. Faith, hope and love is core to this process because if no cause is involved that touches people's inner self, reward and production is reduced to a common simple financial trade. No wonder that this makes people cynical about their companies and management and great deeds are only done for a fellow worker or a customer that awakens our deeper feelings of empathy and care - rarely or never for the company.

The very last couple of lines in Habakkuk I am not quite sure how they fit in. However in the business perspective I again see the need to stop and ensure that the soul keeps pace with the measurable material achievements. Adding a little music helps people relate what they are doing to the deeper meaning of life, without which things may get one dimensional, flat and superficial. The greatest values are to their very nature abstract. We can try to understand them, we can try to align to them and make them work for us, but we can never adequately measure them.

At the same time as it is quite revealing and fantastic to find that the same issues are relevant now as they were 2,500 years ago, one inevitably also runs up to the question: When will we ever learn? And this only further underscores that we mustn't be blinded by the goal - the goal doesn't exist, all that exists is the road and that the road is pursued with faith and hope. It is our responsibility and task to ensure it is strewn with flowers of love and keep the thorns of hate well clear of our path.

36. Zephaniah

Warning of coming destruction, when everything will be swept away from the face of the earth.

Neither their gold, nor their silver will be able to save them (the wicked, the violent and deceitful). 1: 18

Seek righteousness, seek humility; perhaps you will be sheltered. 2: 3

I will remove from this city those who rejoice in their pride. Never again will you be haughty on my holy hill. The remnant of Israel will do no wrong; they will speak no lies, nor will deceit be found in their mouths. They will eat and lie down and no one will make them afraid. 3: 11 - 13

On that day they will say to Jerusalem, do not fear. 3:16

He will take great joy in you, he will quiet you with his love, he will rejoice over you with singing. 3: 17

Associations...

36 Zephaniah

A dramatic account for how anti-social behavior must be discouraged and how truth and loyalty and good citizenship will be promoted and prevail and cause a better life based on love and freedom from fear.

So what does the model society look like? Although described by many authors, i.e. St Augustine in 'The City Of God', and Leo Tolstoy in 'The Kingdom of God is Within You', I have here chosen a few passages from Sir Thomas Moore's Utopia:

"Their doors are never locked nor bolted, so easy to be opened, that they will follow the least drawing of a finger, and shut again alone. Whoso will, may go in, for there is nothing within the house that is private, or any man's own. And every tenth year they change their houses by lot."

I have heard and seen people in Sweden and New Zealand who don't lock their doors. Even more people say that it used to be that way, suggesting perhaps that morals and security have deteriorated. If all signed up for a win-win philosophy, i.e. to never seek advantage at anyone's expense, we wouldn't need any locks at all. To more firmly establish such trend we must widely subscribe to compassion and empathy. Not only is your happiness my happiness, but your unhappiness is also my unhappiness.

It have heard that if you in an Arab home admire something it will be given or offered to you, which is described as some sort of peculiar madness. It isn't madness; it is a display of love and generosity. Generosity breads reciprocity, and thus more generosity - the virtuous circle. My friend, the head of mission - in this case an American - of the World Bank in Nairobi had a painting, which my wife admired and said she really liked. You guessed it! And it still graces our home and reminds us of a life long friendship. Without knowing about the gift of the painting we had a beautiful antique bras birdcage that he had admired. By coincidence, on the day of our departure function, these wrapped gifts were exchanged.

"Though they carry nothing forth with them, yet in all their journey they lack nothing. For wheresoever they come, they be at home."

Virtually all cultures promote friendship to strangers and travelers. This natural instinct may have been severely dented by Vandals and Barbarians, Huns and Vikings and conquistadors and other marauders and imperialists, who operated under a grab -and-run-and-exploit (sometimes including murder and torture) philosophy that understandably challenged the wisdom of generosity. However, a hospitable approach to foreigners and visitors has survived hundreds of years of such challenges to be essentially true today as well. Perhaps better education and increasing understanding and communication have assisted in this process.

"No supper is passed without music. Nor their banquets lack no conceits, nor junkets. For they much inclined to this opinion: to think no kind of pleasure forbidden, whereof comes no harm."

"It is extreme madness to follow sharp and painful virtue, and not only to banish the pleasures of life, but also willingly to suffer grief, without any hope of profit thereof ensuing."

"Felicity rests only in that pleasure that is good and honest. Virtue is defined as life ordered according to nature. For when nature biddeth thee to be good and gentle to others, she commandeth you not to be cruel and ungentle to thyself."

Very simple and straightforward logic! All forms of enjoyment are admissible as long as they are not infringing on someone else's joy or happiness. Another issue is that tact and good judgment is necessary in determining what is innocuous in relation to fellow man, and woman. And, yes, let the music in. Lovely music is a true delight for body and soul.

Inducing happiness requires that you like yourself. If you don't like and accept yourself, how can you role model joy and be generous to others?

"And the seventh part of all these things they give freely and frankly to the poor of that country. The residue they sell at a reasonable and mean price."

No one in his right mind can be opposed to supporting people in need. Not only is it generally considered virtuous, any right thinking person must understand that it is in everybody's self interest. This needs no further elaboration.

"Nature as a most tender and loving mother, hath placed the best and most necessary things open abroad; as the air, the water, and the earth itself; and hath removed and hid fartherest from us vain and unprofitable things like gold and silver."

"Though no man have anything, yet every man is rich. For what can be more rich than to live joyfully and merrily, without all grief and pensiveness."

Consider what really counts, what the eternal values are, what our children for generations to come will give us most credit for, for sparing and nurturing. It is unlikely to be antique furniture or ornaments or jewelry, gold or silver. It will be the mountains and the birds, the sunrise and the snowflakes, the fish in the rivers and watching the ocean waves rolling in. It will be friendship, love and intimacy. Children playing! Pandas and elephants. I think all agree this is obvious, but still so many of our pursuits seem to run contrary to this common wisdom.

"How much better it is to lack no necessary thing than to abound with overmuch superfluity."

The beaches and the stars, the sun and the meadows, the lights at night, the moving conversation with the florist, the grace of birds, the ability to enchant with good countenance, the affection of a child or an animal asking nothing in return - these utter delights of life are available to virtually all regardless of financial status. Utopia is within our grasp.

37. Haggai

When the people only looked after their own houses and neglected that of the LORD, good fortune would not come to them.

Give careful thought to your ways. You have planted much but have harvested little. You eat but never have enough. You drink but never have your fill. You put on cloths but are not warm. You earn wages but, only to put them in a purse with holes in it. 1: 5- 6

You expected much but you see it turned out to be a little. 1: 9

From this day on, from the 24th day of the ninth month, I will bless you. 2: 19

Associations...

37 Haggai

Today is 01012002 – the first day of the second year of the new millennium. The weather again looks quite promising and conducive to a walk to the nearby Meji Shrine to get a bit of a sense of how the Japanese spend their time appointed for the soul. As the Shrine is but twenty-five minutes walk away it makes a very reasonable excursion by foot. Looking at my watch, reading 9.00A.M, and not expecting family and guests to rise until an hour and a half later, I decide to take my bike and go and have a look. It is a bit chilly, but with my grey leather jacket from Hampstead, my winter gloves from Stockholm, the red cap I bought at Galeria Petronas in Kuala Lumpur and my comfortable Mephisto shoes from New York, riding my Renault bicycle, purchased in Singapore, the ride proved a pleasure and a breeze.

It was already quite crowded at the shrine. The many temporary kiosks selling mementos and food and drink were all busy and looked like they might have operated all night. There are plenty of police and guards around. This is a bit astonishing in Japan that all seem so well behaved and yet the police force is always out in great number. With so many people on the move I guess you just cannot afford that things get out of hand or become unruly. Everything is very peaceful, children, youngsters, parents, aged - all seem to be coming out. They solemnly walk up to the temple, say a prayer, throw some coins over the fence and then slowly walk on to a few more days of relaxation before addressing their vows to make the new year a better year. After an hour of impressions, a bowl of vegetable soup, and a few small purchases I am back home for some further notations.

Back to Haggai! 'Give careful thought to your ways - you expected much but you see it turned out to be a little.' I believe the Japanese people have pondered this concept now for about ten years. Why is it, when we are so ambitious and we want advancement and progress that so little is happening and people talk about the 1990's as the lost decade? Perhaps it is also the way we measure success and progress that has gone wrong. After a tremendous recovery, for forty years after the devastations of the war, economic growth has slowed to near zero.

We see headlines in local newspapers like "Japan at a stand still," and "Japan in negative territory again." If Japan, being the second biggest economy in the world and in terms of production, as big as all of the rest of Asia put together, achieves a production level of 99.75 % this year as compared to last year, surely that is not a stand still. After some exuberance and inflated asset prices in the 1980's it may be that we are seeing very successful and skilled economic/ political management insofar as no crash has taken place and the vast majority of people are relatively unaffected by the economic slow down.

So should we be contented with the way things are? Of course not, but this is an eternal truth, and there is no need to panic about a period of correction, reflection and taking stock. Everything is about improving and traveling towards a better order. But we mustn't limit our ambitions to 'economic' growth the way we have been used to. Material welfare is great and a blessing, but even greater is the kindred of the souls. To continue to drive the former at the expense of the latter gets less and less palatable to more and more people. From Tolstoy's War and Peace, which I just finished reading, I quote: 'We are prone to fancy that everything is wrecked if once we leave the beaten path; in fact it is then only that Truth and Goodness are revealed to us. Where there is life there is happiness. We still have much to look forward to.'

Celebrating New Year's eve in Japan this year with so many friends in New Zealand four hours ahead, in Sydney and Melbourne two hours ahead, in Singapore, Hong Kong, Kulala Lumpur and Bangkok one our behind, in Sweden and Switzerland eight hours behind, in England nine hours behind, and in the USA fourteen to seventeen hours behind does take away the childhood magic of 12 o'clock P.M. I remember how we all used to think that at this magic moment something very new was about to happen.

Now I have come to realize that life is a continuum that knows no distinct ends and beginnings. All measures and end of chapters are manmade, a bit unreal and superficial. We found ourselves turning the TV on for a local Japanese concert program to provide the best end of year atmosphere obtainable as a backdrop to the traditional opening of the bottle of Champagne. Last year we had New Year's eve in Kuchin in Kerala, South India, and little did we then expect to be living in Tokyo a year later.

In the Review-of-the-year-programs last night, the thing that inevitably was at the top of the reviews was the September eleven destruction of the World Trade Centre in New York with some 3,500 casualties. Tolstoy's view as expressed in 'War and Peace' would suggest that this occurrence like all others in history is a combination of free will and necessity, i.e. evil acts and the preconditioning for such evil acts. These events are difficult at best to predict and have so many complex and interacting micro causes, that they would seem to happen entirely by chance. Tolstoy writes: 'History cannot take a single step forward without contradicting itself.' Were the events of September eleven inevitable? No! Were they totally unforeseeable? No! When things happen it is for a myriad of reasons.

The ways to reduce the risk for recurrence are to expose evil acts and try to incent people to distance themselves from such acts. To show that crime is unacceptable, but equally important is the introspection, i.e. to consider how to prepare our soil, that of the world and all humanity, for love, compassion and brotherhood rather than their opposites. Again a line of Tolstoy's comes to mind: 'In what is the meaning of loving all mankind, and of self-devotion through love, unless it is loving no one in particular, and living a divine and spiritual life'? To reduce hate and promote love is a delicate task requiring perseverance and compassionate, broadminded, visionary leaders. Do we have these leaders today? Have we had them historically? If, so, what do they look like and how can we ensure that only those embracing universal love and understanding are entrusted with mandates to lead?

How can we ensure that we improve in this respect? How can we promote the things we need to promote, not rushing ahead with one aspect of desirables and forgetting all the others? We must take a holistic approach making sure that the needs of the spirit and soul are given due room and consideration along with the more tangible needs. Wasn't this pursuit of balance in life what Socrates, and St Augustine and Sir Thomas More all were seeking as well? Isn't this what our hearts yearn for? Is this maybe the essence of religion? Perhaps we need to make a greater effort to study philosophy in schools and in business? As reading Tolstoy during the last year has been a great joy for me, I end with another quote from War and Peace: 'As we see things, the standard of right and wrong given by Christ must apply to every human action; there can be no greatness where there is no singleness of heart, no kindliness, and no truth. The most difficult and the most meritorious thing in life is to love in spite of all its undeserved suffering.'

38. Zecharaiah

Shout and be glad, O Daughter of Zion, for I am coming and I will live among you. 2: 10

In that day, each of you will invite his neighbor to sit under his vine and fig tree. 3: 10

Not by might nor by power, but by my spirit. 4: 6

Administer true justice; show mercy and compassion to one another. Do not oppress the widow or the fatherless, the alien or the poor. In your hearts, do not think evil of each other. 7: 8 - 10

Once again men and women of ripe old age will sit in the streets of Jerusalem, each with a cane in his hand because of his age. The city streets will be filled with boys and girls playing there. 8: 4-5

The seed will grow well, the vine will yield its fruit, the ground will produce its crops, and the heavens will drop their dew. 8: 12

Do not be afraid, but let your hands be strong. 8: 13

He will proclaim peace to the nations and his rule will extend from sea to sea. 9:10

The flock of his people will sparkle in his land like jewels in a crown. How attractive and beautiful they will be. Grain will make the young men thrive and new wine the young women. 9: 17

If you think it best, give me my pay; but if not, keep it. 11: 12

Associations...

38 Zecharaiah

I don't know why it is divine to sit under a fruit tree or vine. But I know it is by personal experience. Maybe it is the magic of seeing wonderful things coming out of seemingly nowhere, the miracle of growth and birth, to the delight of man and beast. As you spot the fruits you see the white summer clouds and some blue sky through the leaves bringing it home to you that the fruits are expressions of heaven, divine products nurtured by rain and sunshine. The Japanese word for tree is KI which also means mind / spirit.

It is the insignificant things that are important! Consider this passage which seems so simple and trivial, but which somehow captures what life is about, the true highlights.

'Once again men and women of ripe old age will sit in the streets of Jerusalem, each with a cane in his hand because of his age. The city streets will be filled with boys and girls playing there.'

To sit tranquilly in the street, feeling a soothing breeze, chatting, and just looking at the street life, leaning on your favorite cane! And not far away children are playing although it is getting on a bit. They are allowed to be out and about after dark. Who cares if it's late? Some vague music can be heard in the distance. The little shop is still open. There is a chess game going on across the road. A woman dressed in black is sitting on a chair, knitting. Not much light but the mystique of the night. Time stands still. This is life. Precious moments! There is a scent of compassion, love, low-key contentment and eternity.

If you want to pay me, do, but if not, so be it. The price really isn't what you are charging but what someone is willing to pay, reflecting perceived value. For sustainable business relationships, there cannot be any other way. Honesty boxes work. In New Zealand there are plenty of farmers selling vegetables and fruits on that basis. You take what you want and then you deal with the cash box yourself. It feels beautiful and it works.

If you get too smart and try to get more than you pay for or pay less than true value, it will catch up with you. You are eroding your good will. And as modern corporations well know, good will is the biggest value of virtually all entities that trade profitably. Consciously eroding good will is bad economics, like shooting yourself in the foot.

It may look like underpaying staff is good for profits. Think again. If you are trying to pay 80 percent of market you are likely to get 70 percent of capacity or value. If you pay peanuts people start to act like monkeys. Discretionary energy and a desire to innovate and succeed can only be triggered from within. In that sense a large part of applied labor and energy really is voluntary. People are pretty smart generally and having smart people should certainly be your preference. If you try to fool smart people, you can bet your bottom dollar that you are not going to get away with it. You are embarking on a steady route to decline. Believe me, I know. There are few things so well understood by individuals as comprehending the value of their contribution.

And yes, if you haven't been to Jerusalem yet, go. Just walk around slowly, look at the walls, the narrow streets and the mix of people. Breathe the air and ponder the worries, hopes and dreams of man, woman and child through the millennia.

39. Malachi

About falsehood, blemished sacrifices and false priests and the Day of Judgment.

Cursed is the cheat. 1: 14

True instruction was in his mouth and nothing false was found on his lips. 2: 6

Guard yourself in your spirit, and do not break faith with the wife of your youth. 2: 15

I hate a man's covering himself with violence. 2: 16

You will again see the difference between the righteous and the wicked. 3: 18

You will go out and leap like calves released from the stall. 4: 2

Associations...

39 Malachi

Trying to get ahead at someone else's expense isn't going to work. An innocent digression once or twice is perhaps not going to hold you back, but making it your way inevitably will catch up with you and tax your future. When your surroundings perceive your lack of truth and values, they will understandably and rightly avoid supporting you and doing business with you until you change your ways. Bending rules is different. Rules must be challenged and tested and when obsolete they need to be abolished, adjusted or changed. Because of leads and lags we sometimes need to operate ahead of such changes.

We must never be upholder of rules and instructions only, but need to reflect on what is just and best, as long as our actions are not contravening truth and transparency and our common concepts of love and compassion. Any officer who is merely an upholder of rules has traded away his or her God given right and obligation to exercise judgment. The more laws and rules the less justice. However, challenging rules is diametrically opposed to acting in bad will, i.e. cheating.

Transparency and honesty is part of all religion as their opposites quickly erode the foundations of the community. Voice your opinion, comment on your goals and achievement regularly and openly and you will stay free from reproach. I have made it a habit since many years back to report to my staff, those who I have been set to serve, in writing every month conveying achievements and other pieces of information that may feed and nurture the soul. Copying this multi input report - I also ask others responsible for groups of staff to contribute a paragraph or two - widely to other interest holders, means that I don't have to do much more reporting. All the numbers are usually captured anyway by the significant accounting and IT structures that exist in every modern organization.

But for most people numbers alone are not enough to make them elated. An interesting line on this topic can be found in Tolstoy's War and Peace from which I quote: "Before engaging in the investigation of the chemical qualities of manure or in calculations of 'debit and credit' he took pains to ascertain the number of stock held by his peasants and did everything he could to increase that number. At seed times and hay and grain harvests he paid equal attention to his mojiks' fields and to his own: with the result that few owners had fields so well sown and reaped, so richly profitable, as had Nicholas. Every order of his, he knew well, would meet with the approval of the majority of them, even though one or a few should complain." The human condition remains basically the same. Care and compassion meets with approval, respect and loyalty.

We should try to avoid separation and divorce. The risk if we take our vows too lightly is that we become more miserable, not less, and that we create mistrust and instability. I grant that under certain circumstances it may be best to part ways, but often it seems done in haste and without due consideration of consequences for those involved. To improve the survival rates of marriages we should consider not tying the knot too early and not give up our outside life but each keep up old friendships. We need to ensure that there are some common interests and try to show a bit of love and compassion. Why is it important? It helps build stability and harmony and sets the example that we shouldn't run away from our commitments. And as Tomas Lynch very eloquently points out in is book 'Bodies in Motion and Rest:' "In the wars of divorce it is the children that pay the piper. To have good reasons for divorce doesn't make it good. What good to have your mother's eyes, when your father doesn't love them?"

All violence is evil. I have talked to that elsewhere herein. Make love, not war. And on right and wrong, speak up! Protest! Don't go along. Either you have integrity enough to see and speak up against what is happening or you are part of the problem. There is no room for sitting on the fence. No ambiguity. Stand up to be counted. This is love, this is life and this is concern for the future. 'Go out and leap' on the morrow, greet all you meet with a smile and wish them well, look for situations where love can be demonstrated in practice. Starting a Tsunami or a Mexican Wave of love and care! This is the Utopia available to all of us. Today!

THE NEW TESTAMENT

VI Matthew through Colossians with Associations

1. Matthew

First go and be reconciled with your brother, then come and offer your gift. Settle matters quickly with your adversary who is taking you to court. *5: 24 - 25*

Love your enemies and pray for those who persecute you. If you greet only your brothers, what are you doing more than others? *5: 44-46*

Do not worry about tomorrow, for tomorrow will worry about itself. Each day has enough trouble of its own. *6: 34*

Do not judge, or you too will be judged. For in the same way as you judge others, you will be judged, and with the measure you use, it will be measured to you. Why do you look at the speck of sawdust in your brother's eye and pay no attention to the plank in your own eye? *7: 1 - 3*

Ask, and it will be given to you; seek and you will find; knock and the door will be opened to you. For everyone who asks receives; he who seeks finds; and to him who knocks, the door will be opened. *7: 7*

So in everything, do to others what you would have them do to you, for this sums up the law of the Prophets. *7: 12*

A farmer went out to sow his seed. As he was scattering the seed, some fell along the path, and the birds came and ate it up. Some fell on the rocky places, where it did not have much soil. It sprang up quickly, because the soil was shallow. But when the sun came up, the plants were scorched, and they withered because they had no root. Others fell among thorns, which grew up and choked the plants. Still other seed fell on good soil, where it produced a crop - a hundred or sixty or thirty times what was sown. *13: 1- 8*

If a blind man leads a blind man, both will fall into a pit. *15: 14*

What good will it be for a man if he gains the whole world, yet forfeits his soul? *16: 26*

Many who are first will be last, and many who are last will be first. *19: 30*

Whoever wants to become great among you must be your servant. The Son of Man didn't come to be served, but to serve. *20: 27 - 28*

Whoever exalts himself will be humbled, and whoever humbles himself will be exalted. *23: 12*

Whatever you did for one of the least of these brothers of mine, you did for me. *25: 40*

Associations...

1. Matthew

Such a tremendous change, going from the Old Testament to the New; a true uplift and rejuvenation. Like going from winter to summer, from darkness to light, from fear to love.

To give of yourself and your time is more impressive than offering money. It isn't possible to buy forgiveness or peace of mind. It has to be earned by a commitment to ethics, to fairness, to compassion and love. Creating adversity to gain little will often make you pay more than being gentle and considerate in the first place. The thing that needs to be taken into account is the good will effect. If you win an argument but run down your goodwill, you may well have paid a high price and achieve a Pyrrhic victory. The safest way to build good will is through generosity and compassion and the surest way to run it down is to make gains at the expense of others.

Many people make it their mission to have others concerned and uneasy about tomorrow. Prophets of doom. But tomorrow never comes. We must learn to live in the present, to enjoy the uniqueness of the moment. Time is an illusion. And as much as we need to pay due heed to the future, to foresight and our children, if we make it the sole purpose of our endeavors we are mistaken. Children don't look for sacrifices; they look for happiness, a warm and friendly smile, a hug and some tucking in at night. Some think they are not doing it right if they don't chastise themselves. They are wrong. That's just a weird form of egoism.

Private financial advice is big in Singapore and in Tokyo too as I subsequently found out. The financial advisers (usually from some tax haven) want you to defer income, to store up, no matter how much you have saved, because that is how they make their money. Trying to instill fear instead of love! My advice is not to take too much out of your active lives and use your money when you need it. There must be a balance of living well now and deferring life to a distant future you may not live to see. Someone said that too many men work exceedingly hard for their wives' future husbands.

The same way as you judge others, you will be judged. Bertrand Russell says in The Conquest of Happiness: "It is unlikely that others will think better of you than you think of them." And John Ruskin says "Differences infinite of luster there must be but even the simplest among you has a gift so precious, that, if properly nurtured, he will be a credit to his race." And the same thing is beautifully expressed by the Indian philosopher Swami Vivekenananda: "Let every man and woman and child without respect of caste or birth, weakness or strength, hear and learn that behind the strong and the weak, behind the high and the low, behind everyone, there is that Infinite Soul, assuring the infinite possibility and the infinite capacity of all to become great and good." Don't write anyone off. In every acorn there is the potential for a mighty big tree.

If you want others to act lovingly toward you, make a real effort to find out what is lovable about them. And make them feel it, make their day. The majority of people have some endearing quality about them. When all are going out of their way to try to add quality to the life of others we are well underway to Utopia and the model society. This isn't necessarily that far off. A huge and growing number of people already think in these terms. All good forces relentlessly need to build on this positive approach to life.

All your plants won't bear fruit. Is that a reason for not tending to your garden? If what you are doing is basically right and you harvest multiples of what you have sown, don't feel discouraged by some marginal disappointment. Just try again a second time, and a third time, and a fourth time, and you will find that you will get closer and closer to your goal as you continue to try.

There are now so many books on leadership, but the core of it is recorded in Mathew 20: 27-28. True leaders are the servants of their people keeping the weal of the people at the forefront at all times. "He didn't come to be served, but to serve." The concept of serving is used in modern times in the context of serving a term, serving a constituency and it must be equally natural to serve staff and the public as serving customers. When I had lunch with Sir Sigmund Warburg, the founder of the Investment Bank that bore his name, in London in the 70's, he, despite his phenomenal success and being way beyond normal retirement age, personally served me and one other guest coffee. What a terrific thing to do and what a way to show other staff that our job is to look after our customers and no one is too senior or important to serve and all other human beings deserve a degree of respect.

When you extend a helping hand to someone in need you are helping mankind. A friend in need is a friend in deed. Empathy is contagious. Changing the world for the better in this context is not so much about convincing others to recognize compassion or reason. It is about you and me demonstrating love in action. To do will always be ten times as effective as just to promulgate. The future is ours, shaped by us and enjoyed by us. In the good society all people enjoy the fruits of their labor.

2. Mark

S till others, like seed sown among thorns, hear the word; but the worries of life, the deceitfulness of wealth and the desire for other things come in and choke the word making it unfruitful. *4: 19*

Whatever is hidden is meant to be disclosed and whatever is concealed is meant to be brought out into the open. If anyone has ears to hear, let him hear. *4: 22 - 23*

He took her by the hand and said to her, "Talitah koum!" - Little girl, I say to you, get up! *5: 41*

Nothing outside a man can make him unclean by going into him. Rather it is what is comes out of a man that makes him unclean. *17:15*

To love your neighbor as yourself is more important than all burnt offerings and sacrifices. *12: 33*

Associations...

2. Mark

This week on Wednesday 28th November 2001, two extraordinary things of similar nature occurred. My wife woke up and went to her little back pack to look for her watch. Not there! She realized she had lost it the day before. When at the Yoga class at Shibuya (Tokyo) it is mandatory to take it off and she had stuck it in her backpack in the same fold as her wallet. After the Yoga she didn't put it on but went to three shops on her way back to get a few things. She felt that the watch must have dropped out unnoticed when she pulled her wallet out to pay at one of the shops. She had all the receipts with phone numbers and suggested I ask my secretary to call the shops to ask for it. The reason she didn't do it herself was that the shop assistants in Tokyo often don't speak other than Japanese.

My efficient colleague soon called all the places with little success but they all wrote down the phone number to be able to call back should the watch be found.

This was a really expensive 'Cartier' watch so we also thought of contacting the insurance company. I didn't hold out too much hope there, as we hadn't itemized any of our insured goods at the time of insurance and in addition, clearly if you just loose it yourself there is the issue of lack of owner's prudence. I also thought that perhaps she doesn't really need such an expensive watch so maybe she can find another nice looking watch locally. She had said however that of all her 'things' that watch was the one thing she most cherished. Having paid a small fortune that week for my son's odontologist treatment over six months, and the price of the Cartier watch roughly equaling that expense, I felt that if I can pay for the one, I can pay for the other. Just cough up and get it over with and keep all smiling. It is only money after all and I don't want to die rich.

At two o'clock in the after noon she called and told me that someone from the Yoga institute telephoned and said they had her watch and she could pick it up at her next lesson tomorrow. Happy day! What a relief and how beautiful the world is where honesty is greater than the temptation to walk away with a found precious watch.

When driving home later in the day, I got a phone call from Linda on her way to meet our son who would be arriving that night from Auckland. She said that something much worse than loosing the watch had just happened. So I asked her whatever that might be. And she said that on her way to the Airport-Bus stop she had asked our son Andre' to put her wallet - quite a big lady's wallet - in the front pocket of his American sweatshirt. Suddenly he stopped and said the wallet wasn't there anymore!! It must have fallen out somewhere on the street. Searching for it for twenty minutes yielded no result. And now she must continue that she not be late at the bus stop. The wallet contained three driver's licenses, several credit cards, a cash card, many IDs and club cards and a large amount of money. Japan is still very much a cash society and people carry a lot of cash. What to do? So I suggested she send Andre' back home and look for it on the way and proceed to the bus stop where I would be in twenty minutes.

When I arrived there I quickly found her, she said the bus had just been there but no Felix so he must be on the one-hour-later bus. I thought that if someone finds the wallet, would they be able to identify its owner and location? The only Tokyo location registered was the apartment hotel we stayed at for the first thirty days after our arrival as that address was registered on our official Japanese ID card. So I called that hotel and talked to the very charming and helpful receptionist and she would be only too pleased to help and call us if anyone called them to get in touch.

Linda said that someone may use her credit cards, especially since in Japan you can shop without signing your card purchases if they are below a certain level. Thus she should probably make a police report - did I know where the Shibuya police station was located? Yes I did - it is only three hundred meters down the road. I thought she probably would need a bit of support at the Police station, given that she had no ID at all, so we best go together. Many of the cards she lost I had the match of in my wallet so it would make sense for me to be there for that reason as well. Then Felix suddenly arrived and we decided to drive to the police station to get the report lodged. I guess we all the time thought that there was a better than fifty percent chance that someone will turn the wallet in - maybe without the money, but that is the smaller worry anyway compared with the hassle of renewing all the documents.

Driving back to the Police station on Roppongi Dori I would have to make a U-turn somewhere to get to the other side of the street, and it can take a long time to get to the right spot in the evening traffic. Very soon did I come upon a suitable u-turn place with big No U-turn-signs and given the extraordinary circumstances, and deeming it safe, I used that opportunity. Hard to park of course, but I left the car at the side of the road, rather out of the way and told Felix to sit in the driver's seat and move the car a little if required for any reason. Then into the police station - Linda felt they looked a bit unprofessional in relaxed clothing, but I reminded her that they were helpful and friendly and that goes a long way. After about thirty minutes there, filling out forms, we were ready to go home. The last thing they said was that this was a preliminary after hours report and a proper report would have to be made tomorrow during office hours, which Linda found a bit silly. Half way back to our home, Linda left the car to backtrack her previous walk to look for the wallet once again. I had a hard time understanding that such a big wallet could be dropped without noticing, but no use thinking much about that.

At this time we were quite exhausted and the first night with Felix who we hadn't seen for a long time was perhaps a bit sordid. Linda cancelled her credit cards. I thought there is the chance that you get them all back - but I guess you still need to take precaution. The next day Linda went to the police station again and called me to ask which our insurance company was? Yasuda Fire and Marine - but I didn't hold out much hope for any brake there. While she is sitting in the police station the police suddenly stop the process and say 'Chotto matte' - just a minute - and after a while come back with her wallet, which has just been turned in by a lady. Everything is in it - and not the Y 40,000 she had reported as cash content but Y 60,000, the higher amount probably there due to her lack of remembering, rather than some benefactor adding another Y 20,000. Happy day!! Second time lucky. Praising the Japanese and their renowned honesty. Whether divine intervention was involved or not, these moments make you feel strongly about brother hood, magnanimity and love. When Linda asked the police how to compensate the finder, they told her that she is obliged by law to contact the finder, but from there on it is a matter of agreement without legal guidance.

As we only had a phone number, it wasn't much use Linda calling herself, but through my colleague we found out that the lady didn't want anything, but my colleague suggested we send some money so I wrote a letter praising her for role modeling such admirable behavior which we would talk about to our friends around the world and I enclosed some tangible token of appreciation as recommended.

The reason why I thought of this story in relation to Mark is the line 'whatever is hidden is meant to be disclosed and whatever is concealed is meant to be brought into the open.' Trust and honesty are fundamental parts of a moral win-win society and it has to be promoted by positive action as often as we can. Love your neighbor as yourself.

In his book 'Trust' the author Francis Fukuyama says: "By nature human beings have obligations to each other. A human being cannot perfect himself in isolation; the highest human virtues, like filial piety and benevolence, must be practiced in relation to another human being. Sociability is not a means to an end; it constitutes an end in itself. Trust and similar values like loyalty and truth telling have real practical economic value; they increase the efficiency of the system, enabling you to produce more goods or more whatever values you hold in high esteem."

If you want to make a man trustworthy, trust him. Exhibit yourself, what you wish others to do. This is not so much religion as universal common sense.

3. Luke

L ove your enemies, bless those who curse you, and pray for those who ill-treat you. If someone strikes you on one cheek, turn to him the other also. *6: 27 - 28*

If you love (only) those who love you, what credit is that to you? Even sinners love those who love them. And if you do good (only) to those who do good to you, what credit is that to you? *6: 32 - 33*

Do not judge and you will not be judged! Do not condemn, and you will not be condemned. Forgive and you will be forgiven. Give and it will be given to you. *6: 37 - 38*

Whoever is not against you is for you. 10: 50

And you experts in the law, woe to you, because you load people down with burdens they can hardly carry, and you yourselves will not lift a finger to help them. *11: 46*

Be on your guard against all kinds of greed; a man's life does not consist in the abundance of his possessions. *12: 15*

Do not set your heart on what you will eat or drink; do not worry about it. *12: 29*

From everyone who has been given much, much will be demanded; and from the one who has been entrusted with much, much will be asked. *12: 48*

When you are invited, take the lowest place so that when your host comes, he will say to you, "Friend, move up to a better place." Then you will be honored in the presence of all the other guests. For everyone who exalts himself will be humbled, and he who humbles himself will be exalted. *14: 10*

If he lays the foundation and is not able to finish it, everyone who sees it will ridicule him. *14: 29*

Use worldly wealth to gain friends for yourselves, so that when it is gone, you will be welcomed into eternal dwellings. *16: 9*

Whoever can be trusted with little can be trusted with much, and whoever is dishonest with little will also be dishonest with much. *16:10*

The kingdom of God is within you. *17: 21*

Associations...

3 Luke

It is not uncommon that people are obsessed with finding out who their enemies are and spending much time preventing any ill that may be done to them. This inevitably brings about a vicious circle, leading to more and more miserly feelings. The surest way out of this quagmire is *love*. Now we are at the core of spirituality and religion, i.e. to meet any adversity with understanding and love. Perhaps the most important thing to remember out of the sixty-six books of the Bible is that love is invincible. Bodies succumb, but love is eternal. This is religion. It is also very widely held belief among all religions. But might it not backfire? What about my rights and justifiable expectation to be treated correctly? On the odd occasion it may be testing and seemingly futile to offer love, but it is easy to see that the world we want to build will gain enormously if the word love is engraved on all the foundation stones. Repression and harsh correction and violence can only lead to a never-ending spiral of more of the same. The examples abound.

And yet the world is getting better as more people see and understand the merits of love. But it is not a straight-line trajectory. As I write this I hear on the radio some statements from George W Bush, the new American president. He is saying that Iraq's aggression of following American and UK warplanes (that peacefully, fully armed with the most modern means of destruction, regularly fly over their territory) on their radar screens cannot be tolerated as it endangers American lives? It must be stopped by the disbursement of mega explosives. Not condoning the regime in Baghdad is one thing, but it must be hard for others to see where love and understanding and building for the future is hidden in this equation. Any benefit in disgracing Iraqi leadership must surely be surpassed by what looks like *detournment de povoir*, the misuse of power, and thus loss of good will amongst other countries near and afar. We must not be too narrowly focused on how to correct a perceived immediate ill, but stand back and try to understand what examples we are setting and want to set. We must ensure that the cure isn't worse than the disease. I hope and believe that a better formula can be developed and that this happens sooner rather than later.

The lines from 11:46 on lawyers are interesting 'loading people down with burdens they cannot carry.' And it is rightly placed in connection with love and understanding. So many lawyers, it seems, like to professionally exaggerate the differences and seek to fuel disagreement for financial gain. The cost inflicted on society by the legal profession in the USA, where the problem is most pronounced and basically out of control, is just formidable. And the public pays through insurance premiums for more expensive goods and services and more inertia in government and business. Many worthwhile professions and businesses are threatened to their existence by this litigation madness. In many cases today, whether guilty or innocent, it just makes commercial sense to pay, because the process of winning and clearing your name will set you back much more than an early settlement. The road to turning this problem right will no doubt be long, gradual and arduous, but again the only way is to appeal to integrity, civility, compassion and love. And, in addition, trying to make laws conducive to social behavior and sensible outcomes and practices.

Worrying only about your next meal, life is down to animal level and worrying only about money and possessions is not much better. We owe it to humanity and to ourselves to try to lift the level of participation in life for all, by ensuring freedom from want. We must be sincere about expanding health and education, self-reliance and dignity. It is rarely in our interest to do anything that hurts others. It is almost always in our own interest to do things that benefit others.

Understated is better than overstated. Try to be more than meets the eye rather than less. Pretension always backfires. Common wisdom about the importance of first impression must be taken with a pinch of salt. The best gold is that which is hidden under the surface. Flaunting it leaves nothing to the imagination and it is our imagination that provides the soil for our dreams. The kingdom of God is within you!

4. John

In him was light and that was the light of men. The light shines in the darkness, but the darkness has not understood it. *1: 4 - 5*

Flesh gives birth to flesh, but the Spirit gives birth to spirit. *3: 6*

Everyone who does evil hates the light, and will not come into the light for fear that his deeds will be exposed. But whoever lives by the truth comes into the light. So that it may be seen plainly that what he has done has been done through God. *3: 20 - 21*

The world cannot hate you, but it hates me because I testify that what it does is evil. *7: 7*

If any one of you is without sin, let him be the first to throw a stone. *8: 7*

Walk while you have the light, before darkness overtakes you. The man who walks in the dark does not know where he is going. *12: 35*

No branch can bear fruit by itself; it must remain in the vine. *15:4*

My command is this: Love each other as I have loved you. Greater love has no one than this; that he lay down his life for his friends. *15: 12 - 13*

A woman giving birth to a child has pain because her time has come; but when her baby is born she forgets her anguish because of her joy that a child is born to the world. So with you: Now is your time of grief, but I will see you again and you will rejoice, and no one will take away your joy. *16: 21 - 22*

Blessed are those who have not seen and yet have believed. *20: 29*

Associations...

4. John

Let there be light. Show your honest face, that benevolent countenance that invites transparency and mutual trust. In discussions, show your open palms demonstrating - this is what I think, please let me know if you see it differently - and we can talk about it. Where there is light, humility and communication the risk for misunderstanding, deception and wrongdoing is substantially reduced. Only where there is light can we be sure of taking the right path and avoid the pits, traps and quicksand.

The Spirit is supreme. The Spirit is intangible. The Spirit is immortal. In the spirit dwells everything that is positive and beautiful. The Spirit allows us to stay beautiful and eternally young. It reflects through the eyes. The sparkle is not subject to aging or exclusive to gender or race. Let's make it a priority to nurture and refine our spirits, to try to think and do only that which is constructive and loving. The Spirit thrives on being connected, connected to the world and other spirits. The wider we cast our net, the more inclusively we think of other people, of everything living, the healthier and more shining becomes the Spirit. No branch can bear fruit by itself; it must remain in the vine. Without linking up with others in thought and action we inevitably wither away.

We must have the courage to speak up against wrongdoing. In this process we must exercise care not to become hating and vengeful ourselves, which would be prone to fuel agony and further mistrust. But there is always a way to be constructive and honest and yet true to integrity and sincerity of heart. Often the asking of questions is more useful than condemning or expressing firm views. When a question is asked so that almost any audience, with even the smallest belief in the future and love, would have to answer it in a certain way, even the most aggressive and blinded may see that his position is untenable and reconsider his views and ways.

The asking of questions demonstrates willingness to listen to other views and also is less likely to produce defensive reactions than the coming through with very strong views. There is always the chance that other people's understanding and ideas are as good as or better than ours. Asking questions therefore may afford some useful learning as well. Alan Greenspan, the long serving, legendary Chairman of the Federal reserve Board, said when the market was exuberant: "We must ask ourselves, is the market overpriced"? rather than stating it as a fact, which may have precipitated great turmoil. Even when you are mild and loving, some may hate you and see you as a threat for exposing their evil ways. But if we stop speaking and acting for a better more loving way all hope would fade away and we would cease to be alive.

A rough patch is by definition limited and holding promise of something better. No life is free from challenges, sorrow and disappointment. But no matter what, there is always a new sunrise, a new day holding out the possibility that things be changed and we may be rewarded for holding out. Ganbatte Kudasai! Hang in there! That your spirit may continue to grow and nurture the root of fresh and loving humanity. Beauty and love may withstand even the harshest test and come out more shining and convincing.

Blessed are those who have not seen and yet have believed. "What does reason know? Reason knows only what it has managed to learn (some things perhaps it will never learn; this is no consolation, but why not say it anyway), while human nature acts an entire whole, with everything that is in it, consciously and unconsciously, and though it lies, still it lives. One need only love and have courage." (Fyodor Dostoevsky)

The long New Year's brake is coming to an end and our overseas visitors have left. Back to normal. Gather energy for making the most of the new year. It feels a bit like Monday morning with a long week ahead. But once into it, the tension goes away and we become absorbed with events and options. The sun is slowly rising to a new day of clear blue sky. Trying to make a difference for someone every day, trying to use the allotted time to advantage. Treating all gently and with respect. Avoiding excess of food and drink and any other excesses. Reminding myself of the virtue of humility. These are my aspirations.

5. Acts

All the believers were together and had everything in common. Selling their possessions and goods, they gave to anyone as he had need. *3: 44 – 45*

God does not show favoritism but accepts men from every nation who fear him and do what is right. *10: 35*

The disciples were called Christians first at Antioch. *11: 26*

You are a child of the devil and an enemy of everything that is right! You are full of all kinds of deceit and trickery. *13: 10*

All Athenians and the foreigners who lived there spent their time doing nothing but talking about and listening to the latest ideas. *17:21*

In everything I did, I showed you that by this kind of hard work we must help the weak, remembering the words the Lord Jesus himself said: It is more blessed to give than to receive. 20: 35

Repentance should be shown by your deeds. *26: 20*

Associations...

5. Acts

Reading these notes it seems that generosity is the quality that comes through. Although Acts is about more than generosity, i.e. ignorance, intolerance and persecution of believers, the positive concept revealed is generosity and also encouraging action rather than endless talk about what might be done.

I find that the key messages come back again and again. And that is not only repetition in the bible, the common ground between religions seem considerable. One of the key messages I took out of my recent visit to India is that all religious people are really looking to the same God; different religions just represent different paths to reach the summit. I have also come to believe that it is rather futile to try to establish which religion is best and truest as it is a matter of faith and any intolerance violates the very foundation of religion, which is the common message of love. And after reading Tolstoy's 'The Kingdom of God is within you' I am reinforced in my belief that it is the flame in the innermost, which is God and religion. If that divine flame is there, does it matter who lit it or whether it is white, red or yellow?

'God' encompasses the good and the inexplicable, and the inexplicably good that we know we are not only capable of, but which most of us feel a strong compulsion to act out. And when we go astray and don't measure up to our own ideal we feel miserable and this process helps us move in the direction of good and 'God'. As I was walking down the Mount of Olives with my good friend from Scotland on a warm and sunny September afternoon in 1998, I suggested to him that religion is easy - God is good and good is God. Then he asked me if I also hold that sheep are white and white is sheep.

I must admit I felt a bit thrown off course by his obvious logic, but when I later thought about it, the analogy isn't necessarily relevant, and thus I have gone back to thinking the above. I also think that there are so many things that are hidden from human intellect, and I believe that they always will be, until the end of time. To me all those wonders that we cannot really understand also come under the heading of God. One of the lines from Confucius Analects reads: 'To understand Destiny is to know that certain things in life come under the sway of destiny and that it is futile to pursue them.' Give science a million years and it still will not be able to explain love and affection, the colors of a butterfly and tropical fish, the origin and magnificence of birdsong and the amazement of natural beauty in all its form. Everything beautiful is inexplicable, the crest of which is love and human goodness and affection - that is the ultimate good. That is God. A little book published by a Buddhist society in Kuala Lumpur in the 1950's suggests that it is more important to be devoted to good than to God. And if it can be seen as the same thing there is no conflict.

The little book on Buddhism just mentioned was given to me by a wonderful Singapore Chinese man living in the Singapore suburb of Geylang. My wife found him when we needed our Karen Blixen chairs from Mombasa repaired after our many moves and looked through the yellow pages. She brought the chairs to his workshop which was also his home and house. He was quite critical and only worked on pieces he found worthy of his time. If they weren't he would tell the customer in a nice way that it wasn't worth the money and the effort. He loved his work and worked for love and not for money. He did charge but very nominally. He is the 27th generation of his family doing repair of furniture, and he has good track of all his predecessors but now he is the last of the chain, his offspring not interested in carrying on the vocation.

He showed first Linda and later me around and described lovingly each piece in his home. At each of his many workplaces there was an open book, as he would read in between working on furniture; a carpenter-philosopher who would see a deeper meaning in every exquisite detail and pattern in the marble or wood. To us novices he would point out a detail and always say: That makes me happy. The essence of his life seemed to be to find beauty where other people found nothing and rejoice over anything exquisite. Linda said she wanted to be his apprentice and I have subsequently exchanged mail and thoughts with him very regularly and he continues to personify love and inspiration as well as a zest for life. He has the gift of seeing beauty everywhere, and seeing beauty makes him happy. What a simple and divine formula. God is good!

And coming back to generosity, my friend from the Mount of Olives and I traveled through the Cotswold's next January on a sunny and exceptionally mild winter Sunday. As we had about five hours together between two flights of mine, we covered a lot of ground. He told me that his elder brother had a teaching degree but had got a bit tired of teaching. He had been accepted at Oxford for a law education but didn't really have the money to go through with it. My friend, his younger brother, with quite a good job in the City solved the problem. Not by offering him the money. No. He knew that that would never have been accepted. But he suggested that his brother apply for a scholarship from his, the younger brother's, employer. The employer, a foreign bank, had been known to give these out as an act of good will and community responsibility. So the brother filed an application for a four-year scholarship, which was granted - and, by arrangement, fully deducted from the salary of the younger brother. That is love and generosity at its finest, asking nothing for itself, the most precious of Acts. Whatever good I have tried to do over the years pales in comparison. But it provided a shining light of divine direction.

6. Romans

I long to see you so that I may impart to you some of the spiritual gift to make you strong? that is that you and I may be mutually encouraged by each other's faith. *1: 11*

There will be glory, honor and good for everyone who does good. *2: 10*

If you are convinced that you are a guide for the blind, a light for those who are in the dark, an instructor for the foolish, a teacher of infants, you then who teach others must teach yourself. *2: 20 - 21*

You cannot do evil and expect good to result. *3: 8*

We also rejoice in our sufferings, because we know that suffering produces perseverance; perseverance, character; and character, hope. *5: 3*

You are not under law, but under grace. *6: 14*

Your spirit is alive because of righteousness. *8: 10*

Hope that is seen is not hope at all. Who hopes for what he already has? But if we hope for what we do not yet have, we wait for it patiently. *8: 24 - 25*

You do not support the root, but the root supports you. *11: 18*

Do not think of yourselves more highly than you ought, but rather think of yourself with sober judgment. *12:3* We have different gifts, according to the grace given us. *12: 6*

Love must be sincere. Hate what is evil; cling to what is good. Be devoted to one another in brotherly love. Honor one another above yourselves. Never be lacking in zeal, but keep your spiritual fervor. Be joyful in hope, patient in affliction, and faithful in prayer. Share with God's people who are in need. Practice hospitality. 12: 9-13

Live in harmony with one another. Do not be proud, but be willing to associate with people of low position. Do not be conceited. 12: 16

We who are strong ought to bear with the failings of the weak and not please ourselves. *15:1*

Greet one another with a holy kiss. *16: 16*

I urge you brothers, to watch out for those who cause division and put obstacles in your way that are contrary to the teaching you have learned. *16: 17*

Associations...

6. Romans

It is quite amazing how strong an inner voice we all seem to have, advising us to behave well or at least decently in as far as not interfering adversely with other people's just and honest pursuit of happiness. Doing the right thing, or at least trying to do it most of the time, is its own reward in as much as it is pleasing for the soul. And acting in the opposite way has a tendency to take a heavy toll on harmony and well being. If we are way out of bounds we are likely to get into breaking laws and are liable for tangible punishment, but even if we are just awkward, it will prevent us to reach levels of happiness otherwise achievable.

Thus it will always be good advice to be gentle, caring and supportive, thereby building up friendship and brotherhood, without which a pleasant peaceful life is impossible. This is true not only for Jew and gentile but for humanity in general.

When we wish that the world be made a better place, it most often involves others behaving better. They may, but then they may not. The best way to try to influence is not to condemn or instruct, but to lead by example. If you just ensure that you act lovingly, humbly and generously in all situations, that is the best influence and for that you control the inputs and outputs entirely yourself. No one in his right mind doubts that virtue is rewarding.

A most touching example of appreciating learning from adversity is expressed by 5th century author, Ancius Boethius, in his book, The Consolation of Philosophy, written when he was awaiting execution for being too outspoken. Boethius says in the book:

"Bad fortune I think is more use to a man than good fortune. Good fortune always seems to bring happiness, but deceives you with her smiles, whereas bad fortune is always truthful because by changing, she shows her true fickleness. Good fortune deceives but bad fortune enlightens. By her flattery good fortune lures men away from the path of true good, but adverse fortune frequently draws men back to their true good like a shepherd with her crook. Only bad fortune will demonstrate who your true friends are. Had you been untouched by bad fortune you would have been unable to get such knowledge at any price. So you are weeping over lost riches when you have really found the most precious of all riches - friends who are true friends."

Even if we don't normally wish bad fortune upon ourselves or our friends, the way life pans out there will inevitably be elements of bad fortune for us all, and if we strike some early in life it may well help us count our blessings and appreciate the many little miracles around us, and also make us more resilient. Thus what looks like bad news may often turn out to be a blessing in disguise.

Relationships, contracts and laws are more important from the point of what they don't say than what they say. They can never be more than guiding principles, indicating the spirit under which the relationship is to be governed. Spirit can never be entirely captured and codified just as beauty never can be objectively described. Good attempts can be made, but the real thing has to be experienced. If you think you can regulate all the contingencies of human relationships in a contract, you are either a fool or an American lawyer, or perhaps both in combination. If the guiding principle is love and empathy as manifested in the Golden Rule you are on a much sounder foundation. Therefore it is wise to allow the time it takes to establish trust and good will before any important agreement is entered into. Ill will and malice cannot be exterminated by ever so detailed a contract. Just stay away from untrustworthy people.

Hope and vision are key constituent parts of any dream. They determine the intangible part and value of any organization as well as any individual. They are about improvement and betterment and thus, by their very nature, dynamic, as opposed to static. Perhaps the most important part of leadership is articulating hope in an uplifting and spiritual way. When the spirit is convinced, it creates a sense of purpose and the energy released is just formidable.

In "On Life and Letters" published in 1914, Anatole France says: "Our work is far from being ours. They grow in us, but their roots are everywhere in the nourishing soil. Let us admit then that we owe a great deal to everybody and that the public is our collaborator. Let us efface ourselves so that there may be seen in us, not a man, but humanity. We shall be truly great and good only if we address ourselves to many." We are likely to benefit greatly as individuals if we at all times remember that the inputs into whom we are come from so many people and sources and our outputs and contributions are only meaningful in the context of their utility for other people. Trying to get ahead by pushing others down, either directly thorough evil or malice, or indirectly through pride or conceit, can lead only to disaster and misery. In Confessions by St Augustine, the author says: "All things taken together is better than superior things by themselves." All attempts to build successful all star teams fail because the approach makes the stars lose their shine, and that spirit on which success depends, disappear.

If you try to find something positive to think and say about all people, it becomes normative, like planting a seed. Even if it is only half true, half proved, the likelihood that improvement be achieved is so much greater if people are nourished with praise rather than poisoned by curse and critique. C.S. Lewis in his 'Mere Christianity' says: "A real desire to believe all the good you can of others and to make others as comfortable as you can, will solve many problems."

And finally, we should try to be considerate and not do everything we may have the right to do, but be guided by empathy and how it may make other people feel. Unity is stronger than division. The way you and I act can and will make a difference.

7. First Corinthians

Where is the wise man? Where is the scholar? Where is the philosopher of this age? *1: 20*

God chose the weak things of the world to shame the strong. *1:27*

When I came to you brothers, I did not come with eloquence or superior wisdom. I came to you in weakness and fear and with much trembling. My message and my preaching were not with persuasive words, but with a demonstration of the Spirit's power, so that your faith may not rest on men's wisdom but on God's power. *2: 1 - 4*

Renounce secret and shameful ways, do not use deception, and do not distort. *4:2*

Do not take pride in one man over against another. For what makes you different from anyone else? What do you have that you didn't receive? And if you did receive it, why do you boast as if you did not? Already you have all you want. Already you have become rich. *4:6-? 8*

Knowledge puffs up, but love builds up. *8: 1*

Whoever sows sparingly will also reap sparingly, and whoever sows generously will also reap generously. *9:6*

When a ploughman ploughs and the thrasher trashes, they ought to do so in the hope of sharing in the harvest. *9: 10*

Nobody should seek his own good but the good of others. *10: 24*

Love is patient, love is kind! It does not envy, it does not boast, it is not proud. It is not rude, it is not self-seeking, it is not easily angered, it keeps no record of wrongs. Love does not delight in evil but rejoices with the truth. It always protects, always trusts, always hopes, always perseveres. *13:4-7*

And now these three remain: faith, hope and love. But the greatest of these is love. *13:13*

Rather speak five intelligible words than ten thousand words in a tongue. *14: 19*

Bad company corrupts good character. *15: 33*

Associations...

Seven 1 Corinthians

If we are not pulling together we are pulling apart. We don't need to agree on everything, but we do need to respect and love each other and with these criteria met, there is a lot of room for individuality and differences of opinion. Variety is a sign of tolerance without which love is impossible. Within Christianity and other groupings there is sometimes a tendency to despise anyone with a different opinion, questioning the way in which I lead my life. In schools today we bring people up to ever increasing heights of achievement and reasoning capability. Students are all asked to challenge and improve, to contribute to change and progress, to reflect and add value. As the unexamined life isn't worth living, people not taking an open attitude to differences in opinion do themselves and their cause a disfavor.

Sticking to the old when it doesn't make any sense is quite backwards. In this case I am thinking of the passage in 14: 34 that women should remain silent in the churches. Any discrimination against women is not only out of date; it is contrary to everything we know about Jesus' teachings. And such an opinion is futile to hang on to, as we now know that capability to love, learn, understand and contribute follows no gender lines whatsoever. But perhaps the key point is to concede that this was related to the times and no longer has any relevance. There is a risk that many will turn their faces away from the core great and beautiful messages because proponents of religion insist on promoting ideas that are obsolete and blatantly wrong. Trying to discriminate against women is not uniquely Christian. It is prevalent in most cultures and religions and a sign of custom and primitive attitudes. As women give life to all and epitomize love to many I have always seen God as female.

The other two biblical views, which represent obsolete and outmoded thinking concern slavery and homosexuality. Slavery is just not compatible with the higher order of love and compassion and no one in his right mind defends slavery today. And sexual inclination has no bearing whatsoever on whether a person is good and loving and a credit to his community and mankind. With a true commitment to love, compassion and forgiveness we must move away from passing judgment on people who differ from ourselves.

Here I catch myself focusing on the negative when this letter - the 1st letter to the Corinthians - is so well written and positive. The point I am trying to make is not to defend what's obsolete but give light to the many things that never age, that are likely to be as relevant a thousand years out as they were two thousand years ago and today, i.e. to that which is eternal.

"I came not with eloquence or wisdom but with fear and much trembling with a demonstration of the Spirit's power." This is still the best advice you can give to any speaker: Expose your inner self, expose your heart! Avoid every trace of pretension. Be willing to show weakness and be someone who the listener can relate to and recognize as a human being, a good human being who is out to connect souls, i.e. to promote love, values and community spirit. Even if well researched and clearly formulated, if the message lacks passion, it may well fall flat and underachieve in terms of impact. When the listener feels "I want to take this to me, I want to go out and try to change myself and the way I look at things," then the presentation or meeting has maximum impact. "Rather speak five intelligible words than ten thousand words in a tongue." Don't be too sure; be humble. Enlightenment is voluntary, it cannot be coerced; it must come from within. Wisdom is not knowledge but the *pursuit* of knowledge as per Socrates.

Chapter thirteen on love is almost too beautiful to comment on. It stands and shines on its own, now, and eternally. In my first reading of the bible I missed this passage in as far a marking it out as profound and beautiful. Inevitably with a major undertaking there are moments of mind wonder and lapses in concentration. This is the only way I can explain how I didn't mark it out. It came back to me at a wedding of a colleague's in Singapore where it was read out unabridged. And now I hold it to be one of the most beautiful parts of the Book. If we read these few lines on a daily basis and let them influence and drive our conduct each day the world is bound to become a better place. All you need is love!

8. Second Corinthians

We have renounced secret and shameful ways; we do not use deception, nor do we distort. On the contrary, by setting forth the truth plainly we commend ourselves to every man's conscience. *4:2*

We fix our eyes not on what is seen but on what is unseen, for what is seen is temporary, but what is unseen is eternal. *4: 18*

All this is from God, who reconciled us to himself in Christ, not counting men's sins against them. *5: 18*

We have wronged no one, we have corrupted no one and we have exploited no one. *7: 2*

They gave as much as they were able, and even beyond their ability. *8: 3*

Whoever sows sparingly will also reap sparingly, and whoever sows generously will also reap generously. Each man should give what he has decided in his heart to give, not reluctantly or under compulsion, for God loves a cheerful giver. *9: 6 - 7*

I delight in weaknesses, in insults, in hardships, in persecutions, in difficulties. For when I am weak, then I am strong. *12: 10*

Associations...

Eight 2 Corinthians

This morning I have three competing writing requirements wanting to do some notes to 2nd Corinthians, urged to write an article about happiness for a local news paper, and needing to put together a few lines on the case for 'diversity' in my organization. Thinking I would do this particular one last, after reading the lines above from 2ⁿᵈ Corinthians, they made me so happy and elated that I just couldn't stay away. It also seems that these three tasks are closely related and that within the framework of the quotes above I could find good soil for all three.

Looking at the first paragraph 'renouncing shameful ways' I believe the commitment to ethics, both in relation to customers and staff, and anyone else for that matter, has to be a cornerstone for happiness. Competition (from lat *con petire* - to seek together) is fine if we see it as a fun game for the benefit of humanity where a positive spurring-each-other-on approach leads to more and better service by people who are delighting in the challenges of the game. If we are trying to trip the next person up to get our ends, without regard for the effects on the customer/client/public this is sooner or later going to back fire, to sour our day, to render or working career and life shallow and hollow. Why? Because people don't want to be with, or deal with, someone who is only looking for his own personal gain! Who wants to work in a company that is only trying to enrich itself, its officers or its owners? You can count me out! And even those who sign up for whatever reason will probably only work half-heartedly. Our actions and activities must be able to stand the test of consciousness and have some kind of virtue attached to it. Virtue moves men - shame, deception and distortion do not. Any sustainable venture must be able to pass this test: we have wronged no one, we have corrupted no one and we have exploited no one.

Beauty, happiness and love - what else is there - are all intangibles. They cannot be seen or touched as they all represent feelings of joy. Tangibles are means to reach the intangibles. If we start to compromise the intangibles in our pursuit of more tangibles we are destroying the goal that we are so actively pursuing. Clearly this is happening as business schools and science are sidelining basic human harmony and happiness for what? Higher salary, more dividends, approval of narrow-minded analysts or fund managers! If we compromise away that which constitutes life and dignity, genuine friendships, care and affection we have given up all that makes life worth living. What is seen is temporary - what is unseen is eternal. Anything really important like loyalty, love, and compassion belong to the faculty of dynamic spirit and cannot be readily measured. They are not visible other than through the concept of abstract vision.

Giving and forgiving. If we can keep only these two concepts in our minds on a daily basis we are more than half way there to a better society where there is little room for hate and fear. If we grab any chance we find, and if we actively look for such chances, to give of ourselves and our time for the benefit of a colleague, a friend or whoever, we will find others doing the same and we are all underway to something better.

Organizations that demonstrate 'cause' and a commitment to fully align with virtue and ethics will have happier staff, more loyal, more self sacrificing, less prone to come up with unreasonable pay demands, less inclined to theft and sabotage. Just as corruption breathes corruption, slack ethics lead to falsity and deception. If people learn that whatever you can get away with goes, as far as dealings with customers and the public are concerned, they are prone to take the same attitude to their employer. Virtue breathes virtue, deception breads falsity and lies.

If you have more than others it is for distribution and equalization. Generosity and compassion acts like pesticide on hate and violence, and nurture love and brotherhood.

Can we really make the changes necessary? It is not going to happen over night but humanity means striving, striving for something better, where every life is sacred and given a full chance to develop and bloom.

Some of the finest human thinking recorded was by the founding fathers of the USA. I here include a few lines from the declaration of independence, which seems to stand the test of time. This is I believe equally relevant for Government and senior corporate management.

"We hold these truths to be self-evident, that all men are created equal, that they are endowed (by their Creator) with certain unalienable Rights, that among these are Life, Liberty and the pursuit of Happiness. 'That to secure these rights, Governments are instituted among Men, deriving their just powers from the consent of the governed, - That whenever any Form of Government becomes destructive of these ends, it is the right of the People to alter or abolish it, and to institute new Government, laying its foundation on such principles and organizing its powers in such form, as to them shall seem most likely to affect their Safety and Happiness." /from the Declaration of Independence July 4, 1776/

(as to the three words in brackets I learnt in Washington DC that Thomas Jefferson wanted to keep religion out of the declaration but was instructed to add the three words marked above)

So who says one has to comply with these principles also in the corporate world? No, there is no law saying you have to, but any behavior contrary to what people believe in their core, will no doubt come at a cost of lost opportunity or, loss of general momentum, loss of good will, and loss of good staff.

9. Galatians

I t is fine to be zealous, provided the purpose is good, and to be so always and not only when I am with you. *4: 18*

The only thing that counts is faith expressing itself through love. *5: 6*

If you keep on biting and devouring each other, watch out or you will be destroyed by each other. *5: 15*

The fruit of the Spirit is love, joy, peace, patience, kindness, faithfulness, gentleness, and self-control. Against such things there is no law. *5: 22 - 23*

If anyone thinks he is something when he is nothing, he deceives himself. Each one should test his own actions. Then he can take pride in himself, without comparing himself to somebody else, for each one should carry his own load. *6: 3 - 5*

Let us not become weary in doing good, for at the proper time we will reap a harvest if we do not give up. *6: 9*

Associations...

Nine Galatians

The only thing that counts is faith expressing itself through love. Faith in good, faith in virtue, faith in the power of love! It is natural to most parents to be supportive of their offspring, trying to help and correct, whatever the experienced transgression or set back. If we can find it within ourselves to extend this un-compromised, non-discriminatory and forgiving love to all people, we have achieved '*bonus pater familias*' status, Utopia, the City of God, Dharma and Nirvana or the Way. As more people adopt this win-win philosophy, where any gain at someone else's expense is ruled out as immoral and harmful, we are creating a better world, approaching the ultimate good. There is a great degree of commonality in all religions about this ideal and this essence or nucleus is what I perceive to be the main goal and purpose of religion. Outer form and ritual pales away in significance compared to being compassionate and loving.

It is fine to be zealous if our purpose is good. Too often the purpose gets forgotten. We snare ourselves into highly ambitious, lower level, petty goals when lifting the sight a bit would reveal that the chosen road is coming to an end and leading nowhere. We let the accountants take the drivers' seat when they, like historians, should account for what has happened. The measure of the day for businesses is EVA, economic value added. Where is the vision, where are the values, how do you get long-term prosperity through accountants? I don't have any qualms with accountants, but if you put the cart before the horse, don't be surprised if things go backwards rather than forwards.

A majority of humans feel a deep-rooted desire to try to improve the balance between good and evil, love and hate, generosity and greed. There is a temptation, however, to get so concerned with looking after yourself, that you may throw all values and consideration for others over board for shorter or longer periods. Thinking perhaps that once I have all I need for me and my family, I will start to behave more generously and contribute to others. We must learn that now is all there is, that tomorrow will always be in the future. The overall harvest will be greater if we extend a hand and co-operate and the quality of life for all of us can only improve by compassion. And charity isn't about writing checks so much as a compassionate and helpful attitude, to be willing to give of yourself and your time. But won't this allow free riders amongst people and nations to take advantage of our virtue? Yes, but erring on the side of too much compassion is quite unlikely to happen in a hurry, and even if it did, it is infinitely more appealing than erring on the side of rigidity, repression and division. And the good society imbued with caring and compassion, general and mutual friendship and good will, is a much better insurance against suffering and hardship than ill gotten stores full to the brim. Sowing friendship rather than storing up resentment and envy!

If you keep biting and devouring your fellow man you may destroy each other. Any team or group of people will reach its potential only by working in a spirit of co-operation with a genuine desire to see all do a good job. There must be a total absence of alienation and marginalization. Effort is shared and rewards are shared. No one is seen as a tool for someone else's advancement. All are in there to achieve together and share the fruits of the crop. Just getting this part right is half the success of a team and a management task. To ensure there is no infighting and that no one can or wants to claim an undue part of the credit for success.

A spirit of co-operation often allows a lesser team to win over the favorites. This is why New Zealand won the Americas cup some years back. This is, I believe, why a Swedish coach for the English football team might make sense. We must have the clairvoyance to see that one hero doesn't make a team and that a true team spirit of amateurs often will outweigh a group of superior professionals who are lacking in support of each other. Only if all are allowed to stand tall and say, we did it together, will the magic of team spirit be brought to the fore. A group dependent on the superhuman strength of one person is not a team.

But isn't it futile to continue, when, after all these years of trying, we still have so much misery around us? We mustn't underestimate what has already been achieved and continue to build on the good and relentless efforts of all those who have gone before us. Quoting Sir Winston Churchill; 'Never, Never, Never, give up!'

10. Ephesians

I urge you to live a life worthy of the calling you have received. Be completely humble and gentle; be patient, bearing with one-another in love. Make every effort to keep the unity of the Spirit through the bond of peace. *4: 1-3*

We will no longer be infants, tossed back and forth by the waves, and blown here and there by every wind of teaching and by the cunning and craftiness of men in their deceitful scheming. *4: 14*

Each of you must put off falsehood and speak truthfully to his neighbor, for we are all members of one body. Do not let the sun go down while you are still angry. *4: 25 - 26*

Get rid of all bitterness, rage, anger, brawling and slander, along with every form of malice. Be kind and compassionate to one another, forgiving each other. *4: 31 - 32*

Live a life of love. *5: 2*

Have nothing to do with the fruits of darkness, but rather expose them. *5: 11*

But everything exposed by the light becomes visible, for it is light that makes everything visible. *5: 13 - 14*

Sing and make music in your heart and be grateful. *5: 19*

Husbands ought to love their wives as their own bodies. He who loves his wife loves himself. *5: 28*

Associations...

10 Ephesians

Ephesus was the most important Greek city in Ionian Asia Minor, the ruins of which lie near the modern village of Seljoq by the Aegean Sea in the Izmir province of Turkey. Its history is intertwined with the conflicts between Greeks and Persians and between Athens and Sparta and many famous ancients i.e. Croesus, Xerxes, Alexander the Great, Hiracleitus and Sulla and the Roman Emperors, Constantine and Justinian, are connected with it. By the early middle ages the city was no longer useful as a port and fell into decline. The letter to the Ephesians was once thought to have been composed by Paul in prison, but is more likely written by one of Paul's disciples, probably sometime before AD 90 (Source Encyclopedia Britannica).

Paul believed that God is responsible for everything whereas Plato believed that God is merely responsible for good things. Paul believed that in order to find out the mind of Christ you need to look in your own heart, not to consult work of historical references, even one as venerable as the bible. Ephesus and the area around it in Asia Minor were much more than Palestine, the birthplace or nursery of Christianity. If there is any single individual who can be labeled the originator of Christianity it would be Paul (Source: Paul, the mind of the Apostle by A.N. Wilson).

This week I was fortunate to have the opportunity to attend a luncheon with Junichiro Koizumi, Japan's prime minister and Howard Baker, a distinguished seventy-six years old American politician, currently the US ambassador to Japan. Both would no doubt benefit from reading and contemplating Ephesians. Koizumi who enjoys unparalleled popularity with the Japanese electorate, gives the impression of deep sincerity and social awareness and empathy. He is also fully committed to structural reform in Japan, which is needed to get out of the current economic quagmire. Whether he can do it or not remains uncertain but the resolve is there. Why is it so difficult?

The Japanese banks still have a mountain of non-performing loans making them unable and unwilling to lend to new ventures. Full employment is a holy cow in Japan so any change must minimize the impact on employment. Labor laws are incredibly supportive of the employee. Agriculture and construction, distribution and retail are all engaging powerful economic and political groupings, all fearing the unknown and trying to hang on to the past. Whereas the top manufacturers and exporters are world class, these other four economic sectors mentioned, carrying up to 50 % more people than required, are in screaming need for reform and efficiency improvements. The currency parity means that Japanese labor costs are among the highest in the world. Corruption and organized crime is lurking in the background. Political coalitions erode the ability to act firmly and decisively. For every expert saying this is what the country needs, there is another expert saying the opposite. Koizumi is no doubt trying to live up to the calling he has received, making every effort to keep the unity of the Spirit through the bond of peace. But given the challenge it will require a unique combination of skill, resolve and patience.

Howard Baker ex majority leader of the Senate and Chief of staff under president Reagan talked about the need to listen, ask questing and try to understand other people's views. Big countries like the US and Japan, the two biggest global economies, need to try to understand their role in the world and the two countries need to explain themselves to each other. With reference to the September eleven shock, MR Baker said that terrorism must be countervailed wherever found. The situation arising from this incident has brought together countries around the world in a totally unprecedented constellation. He talked about rebuilding Afghanistan and kept repeating the name of that country so many times that I thought he was limiting and confining a problem that is bigger than any country or geographical enclave.

One question appearing in my mind was how honest is a person like this? How does he balance his own view and convictions with instructions and policy handed down from the administration? This is a dilemma most of us are facing and one of the reasons why values and purity of heart and intent are so important. I wanted to ask him what he thinks of President Bush but knew the question would have been naïve and mal-placed. The question I did ask was: 'You mentioned reconciliation a few times in your speech. How do you see this happening, what is required?' He stated that he was an optimist. Unless we think the possible, we only harvest the impossible. Reconciliation requires that we deal to hunger and poverty. It requires that health care and education is available to all. We must allow and support self-determination in terms of how different peoples and countries govern themselves. He said he hoped that ten years out people would say the September eleven two thousand and one was the catalyst for the world coming together. He said he has always believed that 'the best it yet to come.' I thought he did rather well in the end. There is no reason why it shouldn't be that: 'the best it yet to come.'

In an article in the Chicago Tribune this week W J Clinton, the 42nd president of the United States says: 'We have to create more opportunity for those left behind by progress, thus reducing the pool of potential terrorists by increasing the number of potential partners. To make new partners, the wealthy world has to accept its obligation to promote more economic opportunity and help reduce poverty.'

From the letter to the Ephesians I think I know how Paul would have answered my question to MR Baker: 'Get rid of all bitterness, rage, anger, brawling and slander, along with every form of malice. Be kind and compassionate to one another, forgiving each other. Live a life of love.' Knowing what your goal looks like is a good start. But the greater part of achievement is implementation through resolve and dedication and for each individual to role model love; putting love into practice.

11. Philippians

May your love abound more and more in knowledge and depth of insight, so that you may be able to discern what is best and may be pure and blameless. *1: 9-10*

If I am to go on living in this body, this will mean fruitful labor for me. *1: 22*

Do nothing out of selfish ambition or vain conceit, but in humility consider others better than yourself. Each of you should look not only to your own interests, but also to the interests of others. *2: 3-4*

Do everything without complaining or arguing, so that you may become blameless and pure. *2: 14 - 15*

I do not consider myself yet to have taken hold of perfection, but one thing I do: Forgetting what is behind and straining towards what is ahead. *3: 12 - 13*

Only let us live up to what we have already attained. *3: 16*

Let your gentleness be evident to all. Do not be anxious about anything. *4: 5-6*

Finally, brothers, whatever is true, whatever is noble, whatever is right, whatever is pure, whatever is lovely, whatever is admirable - if anything is excellent or praiseworthy - think about such things. *4: 8*

I have learned to be contented whatever the circumstances. I know what it is to be in need, and I know what it is to have plenty. I have learned the secret of being content in any and every situation, whether well fed or hungry, whether living in plenty or in want *4: 11- 13*

Associations...

11 Philippians

Everything is fluid. Life is dynamic and nothing stands still. And yet so much of what we do is based on static measures and clinging on to what has been. John Ruskin says 'For every twenty people who produce well, there is only one who knows how to spend well.' Whatever you have produced, whatever you have earned, it is history. It says very little about your vision, where you are going. This is where your spending skills come in. Whether you spend in a way that erodes your equity or in a way that builds for the future. What is seen is temporary, but what is unseen is eternal. A scale will tell you how much you weigh, but very little about your resolve and method for changing your appearance. The body you can measure but the soul you cannot. And yet the soul is infinitely more valuable than the body. It continuously gains in vigor whereas the body loses out. So what sense does it make to focus our measurements on that which is less valuable and to ignore that which is more important?

Goodwill is the credit you build up with the world around you. This is true for organizations as well as for individuals. That reputation, when well nourished, will always be worth more than any tangible, easy-to-measure, asset. This reputation is strongly based on the desire to do good, to serve better, and to reinvent yourself and to improve in years to come. Love and generosity are its solid foundations. Goodwill is very dependent on ethics. Ethics means willing and doing the good without harm or any ulterior motives. In case of non-compliance with ethics you are on a risky and unsustainable path. Any feeling of complacency, any feeling that we are already very good, and that we can cruise forward and rest on our laurels will necessarily lead to stagnation and decay.

If it needs doing, just do it. A positive can-do attitude is contagious and makes life so much easier for all in a home or an office or any other forum. Get on with it! Why not? But what if it is someone else's job and I have already done mine? Never mind, if you have the strength and ability to deliver over and above norm, just be grateful for this gift. You will never lose out by being helpful and delivering above expectations. On the contrary, it is a recipe for success and building goodwill.

In this context it is desirable that schools and universities try harder to inspire growth of character, attitude, vision, ethics, fellowship, tolerance and love and not only focus on the acquisition of skills. The former 'soft' qualities are at least as important as skills in building relationships between people and ensuring that achievements align with what serves mankind in the long run. If we know what to do, but not why or for whose benefit, the risk that we go seriously astray is obvious. Confucius said that morals are akin to a skill - and skills without morals are like vehicles without engines.

Bits and pieces, fragments! Where is the red thread? It is Sunday in Singapore in April 2001 and so many little things distracting. But fragments may turn out to be a mosaic. Although not fully drawn together, somewhat of a picture may emerge for the reader. This is my hope. Life is a bit like that. An impression here, an impression there and a fuller view can perhaps be sensed. At the end of the day, it is for each individual to try to find cohesion and make some sense of a world full of contradictions and ambiguity.

So many things never get said or written because of harsh self-censure. Sometimes too much gets said because of lack of it. I much liked St Augustine's final comment in the City of God: "Let those who think I have said too little, or those who think I have said too much, forgive me; and let those who think I have said just enough join me in giving thanks to God." And the author of The Little Prince, Anthoine De saint-Exupery said: "perfection is attained not when there is nothing more to add, but when there is nothing more to take away."

12. Colossians

B e encouraged in heart and united in love. *2: 2*
Set your minds on things above, not on earthy things. *3: 2*
Clothe yourselves with compassion, kindness, humility, gentleness and patience. Bear with each other and forgive whatever grievances you may have against one another. And over all these virtues put on love, which binds them all together in perfect unity. *3: 12 - 14*
Whatever you do, work at it with all your heart, as working for the Lord and not for men. *3: 23*
Let your conversation be always full of grace, seasoned with salt, so that you may know how to answer everyone. *4: 6*

Associations...

12 Colossians

Good morning. The working week has come to an end and the two days appointed for spiritual and bodily health have begun. A common thread through Colossians is not to separate work and ideals, daily chores and love, but to have these two intertwined at all times. If we see the vision of where we want to be and what we want to create as we approach our daily tasks - whatever they may be, as long as they are honest and honorable - the chance is that what we do will be brought to a new level and dimension. On my morning walk with the dog I stopped in at the local 'Levain' bakery where five or six Japanese youngsters have something divine going, pouring love into every single piece of bread they make - dark, coarse bread with raisins, nuts and seeds.

Prices are by weight and quite high compared to supermarket bread, but the product is different beyond comparison. You look at the bread and take a bite and the sense of harmony and health experienced in the shop permeates your whole body. No wonder it is popular and drawing lots of repeat business from satisfied customers. Perhaps it is a role model for others? Definitely! Any business, which fails to bring out the spirit and soul of its employees is missing out on the best. And if you have thousands of staff, hierarchically organized I am afraid you are on the wrong track and you will never get there. How can anything be successful if it doesn't generate and align with harmony, happiness and love? It can't. In the book Simple Truths, the author Fulton Sheen says: 'I became lovable because you poured some of your goodness and love into me.' This is true for everything animate and inanimate. Exposure to love creates a special shine.

Trying to check on 'Levain' in my dictionaries and encyclopedia I finding nothing and conclude that it may just be the name of the founder or owner. The closest I get is 'Levant' from the French *lever* 'to rise' as in sun rise, meaning the east and generally referring to the countries on the coast of the eastern Mediterranean. As associations go, from now on, this will add to my sensation and delight in eating the bread - the sense of warmth, energy and excitement that comes from the sun rising to another day. Putting anything on bred like this, i.e. marmalade, cheese, ham, seems like sacrilege. It is complete in its own self. No need to add - no need to subtract. And like true beauty, it doesn't seem to age. This is my daily bread, another blessing there to be enjoyed.

In his book 'As a man thinketh', the author, James Allen says: 'At the command of glad and cheerful thoughts the body becomes clothed with youthfulness and beauty. There is no physician like cheerful thought for dissipating the ills of the body; there is no comforter to compare with goodwill for dispersing the shadows of grief and sorrow.' If this cheerful thought can be nourished and maintained by a group of people who then 'infect' others, customers and friends, with the same spirit, does anyone doubt that you have captured the key component in success? And finally a line by Robert Louis Stevenson: 'If a man love the labor of any trade, apart from any question of success or fame, the gods have called him.'

VII Thessalonians through Revelations with Associations

13. First Thessalonians

We continually remember your work produced by faith, your labor prompted by love and your endurance inspired by hope *1:3*

The appeal we make does not spring from error or from impure motives, nor are we trying to trick you. *2: 3*

We dealt with each of you as a father deals with his own children, encouraging, comforting, and urging you to live lives worthy of God. *2: 13*

No one should wrong his brother or take advantage of him. *4: 6*

Make it your ambition to lead a quiet life, to mind your own business and to work with your hands, so that your daily life may win respect of outsiders and so that you will not be dependent on anybody. *4: 11 - 12*

Warn those who are idle, encourage the timid, help the weak, be patient with everyone. Be joyful always. Avoid every kind of evil. *4: 14 – 22*

Associations...

13 First Thessalonians

Today I read about demonstrations in the Canadian City Quebec. Previously it was Seattle and Davos! Top government leaders are coming together to discuss and promote trade. Why is that causing such angst and concern. Isn't it good for the world if more nations trade more openly with each other?

I think no one in his right mind is against international trade, networking, brotherhood and sisterhood. But if speeding up the economic wheels to create more GDP growth is all top politicians and businessmen are concerned about, that clearly isn't good enough. So the protest isn't about what these people do, but rather what they don't do.

Where is love, where is faith, where is hope for the many? That isn't even on the agenda and that rightly causes disgruntlement. The traditional way of looking at growth often isn't growth at all, but a disguised way depleting assets and stealing from the future and from our children, and sometimes from those countries that can least afford it. This must be changed so as to reflect and guarantee improved quality of life and happiness for the many, and not only the few. You may argue that that is a different issue. Well, if it is, why isn't more attention allocated to it? Growth in trade should be a subdivision of improved quality of life, i.e. growth in care and empathy and providing opportunity for participation and the betterment of living conditions for larger groups of people.

A few lines from the 19th century author John Ruskin refer: "There is no true wealth but life including all its powers of love, of joy and of admiration. That country is the richest which nourishes the greatest number of noble and happy human beings; that man is richest, who, having perfected the functions of his own life to the utmost, has also the widest helpful influence, both personal, and by means of his possessions, over the lives of others." Unless what we strive for and achieve helps also the weak and less fortunate to a share in the advancement, has there really been any advancement at all?

These are real and relevant questions asked by many rich and all the poor people of the world, and unless what we do is seen to align with love, care and empathy - which most of us hold high and claim to promote - we may be wasting our time as well as being seen as hypocrites. If we are a bit intelligent about it, there isn't really a conflict here. Bringing the disadvantaged along creates bigger markets, less risk and agony and thus contributes to universal happiness. It is rarely in our interest to take a course of action, which isn't of general benefit to most, if not all, of mankind.

14. Second Thessalonians

M ay every good purpose of yours be fulfilled. *1: 11*
We were not idle when we were with you; nor did we eat anyone's food without paying for it. On the contrary, we worked night and day, laboring and toiling so that we would not be a burden to any of you. We did this not because we do not have the right to such help, but in order to make ourselves a model to follow. For even when we were with you we gave you this rule: If a man will not work, he shall not eat. *3:7 - 10*

And as for you, brothers, never tire of doing what is right. *3: 13*

If anyone does not obey your instruction, do not regard him as an enemy, but warn him as a brother. *3: 14 – 15*

Associations...

14 Second Thessalonians

Geographically we are in northern Greece in what is today the second biggest city. Thessaloniki, the capital of the northern province of Macedonia, has had more than its fair share of misery and massacres. My own visits to Greece are limited to Athens, Crete and the southern part of Cyprus. In spite of Greece's early cultural dominance, its position next door to Asia Minor and the seemingly eternally fragmented many nations of the Balkans has brought a lot of hardship over the millennia. It's political hey days are but a distant memory. Culturally however, the foundation laid by Greek thinkers will continue to provide much of the basis for human civilization and advancement.

That which has been can never be changed. It is puzzling how moral and intellectual leadership comes and goes between the peoples of the world. The half millennium just before Christ brought out some of the finest thinking the world has seen, not only in the Occident but also in the Orient. The letters to the Thessalonians were written by Paul from Corinth, Greece, about AD 50. The City of Thessaloniki was founded in 316 BC and named after a sister of Alexander the Great.

Mai-Nichi Inu-To Sanpo -Su-Ru-n- Desu. As the dog starts to move around on this Sunday morning, I recall this sentence - *Every day I take the dog for a walk* - from my Japanese studies. Whatever inanimate things may occupy your mind, things animate, calling for attention, must take precedence. As it is pouring down with rain this morning I put on my dry-z- a-bone hat, my oilskin coat and wet weather boots making me impregnable for any unpleasant effects of the rain. Dog isn't as fortunate but always seems keen for a walk anyway. It is really lovely to be out and have proper gear making the walk equally pleasant weather there is sunshine or rain. And, besides love and sunshine, water probably is the most important element for life and days of rain must be welcomed.

For this walk I brought a copy of 'Colossians and Associations' (se above) with a small note in an envelope in my inner pocket, safe from the rain. As I approach the 'Levain' bakery I find that a car is parked next to the pole where I normally tie the dog. As I am about to tie the dog there, it strikes me that the driver may jump into the car without seeing the dog and an accident might happen. So I find another safe place ten feet away.

This reminds me of two 'accidents' I have had with the dog. On Christmas eve - my birthday - 1998 in Auckland, New Zealand, I was asked to go and get a nutcracker at Millie's, the nearby kitchen ware shop. It was a beautiful summer's day and I brought the dog along and tied her just outside the shop on the wide pavement of Ponsonby Road. Christmas commerce was buzzing in the shop so I had to wait about ten minutes to be attended to. Sure enough they have a nice sophisticated nutcracker, quite expensive as I would expect, but if you want quality there aren't any shortcuts.

When I get back to the house in the early afternoon I feel very tired and we are having about twelve people for dinner with singing and games etc so I ask for leave to take a nap. As it is my birthday, I get away with it - otherwise I would be required to assist in the preparations. After an hour's sleep I am awakened by some commotion. So I get up and learn that the dog is missing? All are a bit upset and my youngest son and his friend start to look around the neighborhood in search for the dog. You guessed it! After half an hour they found the dog outside Millie's where kind people had gotten into the Christmas spirit by supplying her with some water to cope with the summer heat. I of course was quite embarrassed being the cause of the incident, but in the spirit of the day, I wasn't reproached but it was seen as another sign of how distrait I sometimes am.

On the second incident, this time in Singapore two years later, I found myself on the inside of our home elevator with the dog outside and the leach connecting us. The door closed and the lift started in spite of my desperate efforts to stop it. I could hear the dog yelp and then the leach snapped and I thought this is the end of the dog as well as any goodwill I enjoy with my family. Quickly returning to ground floor feeling distinctly faint, I found the dog looking a bit shocked but, thank God, physically unharmed.

Back to the bakery! Stepping into the shop, they all greet me as a long lost friend and I get reassured that this place is special. Checking our home breadbasket before I left, I know we don't really need any bread, but with people like this, that is not really an issue. Let's buy some anyway. Utility is of no consequence for love. Love lives on a different plane. I get the loaf in a bag and the little extra piece they always stick in as a 'bonus.' Due to the heavy rain outside I insert the paper bag - no plastics in this shop - under my oilskin coat and start my return walk. I feel the heat of the fresh bread spreading to my body and again think that this is no ordinary heat, this is an effect of the love poured into the product by the bakers.

When on a ski trip yesterday to Gala - about two hours away from Tokyo with the bullet train- reading my book I came across this beautiful passage in Tolstoy's Childhood. The dying mother is writing a letter to her husband and says " You are so kind hearted, my dear one, that for fear of worrying me you conceal the real state of your affairs; but I can guess: no doubt you have lost a great deal at cards and I assure you, I am not at all troubled about it. So if matters can be arranged all right, pray do not think overmuch about it, and don't worry yourself needlessly. I am accustomed not to count on your winnings for the children, nor, forgive me, even on any of your property. Your gains give me as little pleasure as your losses cause me anxiety." Time and again in Tolstoy's writing does he give example of the most beautiful role modeling of love. Reading things like this naturally inspires the thought that when difficulties hit me, may I have the strength to act and think nothing but love. Although people aren't always the way you hope they were, loving whatever is lovable will nurture love rather than resentment. By the way, I couldn't believe how untouched and spectacular a landscape is available just a few moments by train away from Tokyo, the biggest city in the world. A beautiful day of skiing - Japan is fantastic.

Reflecting on my last excerpt from Thessalonians, if, when we instruct or interact with others, our continued respect and appreciation for the other person is demonstrated as solid and firm, whatever his or her opinion, we can try to influence the thinking without causing resentment or animosity.

15. First Timothy

Love comes from a pure heart and a good conscience and a sincere faith. *1: 5*

Don't let anyone look down on you because you are young, but set an example for the believers in speech, in life, in love, in faith and in purity. Do not neglect your gift, which was given you. *4: 12 - 14*

Stop drinking only water, and use a little wine because of your stomach and your frequent illnesses. *5: 23*

For we brought nothing into this world and we can take nothing out of it! But if we have food and clothing, we will be content with that. People who want to get rich fall into temptation and a trap and into many foolish and harmful desires that plunge men into ruin and destruction. For the love of money is the root of all sorts of evil. *6:7-10*

Command them to do good, to be rich in good deeds, and to be generous and willing to share. In this way they will lay up treasure for themselves as a firm foundation for the coming age, so that they may take hold of the life that is truly life. *6: 18 - 19*

Associations...

15 First Timothy

Love, purity and faith! These aims are easy to express and commit to, but difficult to put into practice, consistently, all the time. As long as we have an ideal that we believe in we sense quite strongly when we transgress which encourages us to get back in line.

So what is faith? As a minimum, it is faith in good, in love and conduct that promotes happiness and well being for the many. And in this context we must beware that any group is built up of individuals, so if we start to sacrifice individuals for the benefit of the many we tread a very dangerous course. Love is capable to be extended to all and thus rarely is it right to assume that the end justifies the means. There is no end. There is only a long endless journey, which is made meaningful through love. Subdivisions of love are tolerance and humility, failing which love is superficial and lacking in sincerity.

Sensuality is natural in our make up and it is precious and good. Don't be afraid to love, and make love - without it the world ceases and stops. Sensual intimacy is good and sex is natural when loving and sincere. We mustn't feel bad about this most precious of human experiences. But we do need to keep it in perspective and particularly in this field, be considerate and loving because deceit in something so intimate and core to whom we are can leave irreparable scars. The focus should be in giving rather than taking and never should we indulge in sensuality under any false pretence for one-sided selfish satisfaction. And of course any obsession is likely to take away from the beauty of the experience. Pacing ourselves and looking to balance our lives are key aspects of lasting happiness.

Young or old, each phase has its relevance and its beauty. The body may get a bit frail of aging, but the beauty of the soul does not wither with time. And there is no guarantee that older is wiser. The gift of wisdom, soul, spirit and love can appear naturally even in very young people, who may have an advantage in being less loaded with prejudice and convention. True beauty is in the soul, which expresses itself through the eyes and countenance. A person filled with love and affection never loses her beauty. It is interesting how we sometimes use female pronouns rather than male. But when it comes to these intangible spiritual qualities, if feels very natural for me to use the female gender.

Asceticism is fine if natural and unimposing. If it impinges on the quality of life or if it intolerantly requires of others to go to unnatural extremes, then it too can become a vice. Wine in moderation clearly can add to the quality of life. The wise person always has a glass of water handy and does normally not exceed a couple of glasses of wine at any one occasion. Ignatius Loyola, who lived in the first half of the sixteenth century, advised: 'Provided one takes care not to fall ill, the more one can cut back on one's normal intake, the sooner will one arrive at the just mean in eating and drinking. Above all one should take care not to become wholeheartedly engrossed in what on is eating, and nor be carried away by one's appetite and meals; instead one should control oneself, both in the manner of eating and the quantity eaten.'

Having enough money is a blessing, particularly as it helps you support that which you hold dear and believe in. But the true blessing is when acquired affluence is only a side effect of expressing love through your work and deeds. If you have to compromise your soul or values in pursuing wealth, chances are that you have your happiness formula twisted and you end up in spiritual poverty.

The best most endurable treasure you can store up is the good will you build by looking to express love and support for as wide a circle as is humanly possible. This wealth cannot be taxed and it is immune to inflation and any other erosion.

16. Second Timothy

F or God did not give us a spirit of timidity, but the spirit of power, of love and of self-discipline. *1: 7*

If anyone competes as an athlete, he does not receive the victor's crown unless he competes according to the rules. *2: 5*

The hardworking farmer should be the first to receive a share of the crops. *2: 6*

Present your self a workman who does not need to be ashamed and who correctly handles the word of the truth. *2: 15*

Don't have anything to do with foolish and stupid arguments, because you know they produce quarrels. And rather than quarrel, be kind to everyone and not resentful. *2: 23 - 24*

Keep your head in all situations and endure hardship. *4: 5*

Associations...

16 Second Timothy

This should have been the day of my return from a long trip but in the eleventh hour the trip was cancelled. As the trip would have covered Auckland, Melbourne and Singapore, it held out the promise of seeing a lot of old friends. Many appointments had to be disappointed. Even if the trip didn't happen it gave me the satisfaction of eager anticipation, perhaps the greatest stage of the three, the other two being consummation and remembrance. And I have a new trip scheduled two months out anyway so the net effect is just a somewhat drawn out period of anticipation.

Our delight with anticipation is perhaps why childhood and youth are such cherished stages of life. 'Oh the happy, happy, never to be recalled days of childhood!' How could one fail to love and cherish memories of such a time? What better time in our life can there be than when the two finest virtues - innocent gaiety and a boundless yearning for affection are the only mainsprings of one's life?' says Tolstoy in "Childhood, Boyhood, Youth." Clearly we have to learn to appreciate all the stages in life as each has its particular charm and beauty. The author Tiziano Terzani says in his 'Earthbound Travels in the Far East': "I instinctively always find the past more fascinating than the future, and the present often bores me, so only by thinking of how I will remember it later can I enjoy the moment."

Another view on tenses is expressed by Kafka in 'Contemplation' where he says: 'I compare my past with my future, but find both stupendous, can give neither my preference, and can find fault only with the injustice of the providence that is favoring me in this way.' And to illustrate engrained pessimism, the author Rory Maclean in his book 'Stalin's Nose' (humorously) relates how when a Hungarian is asked how he feels, he responds 'Worse than yesterday but better than tomorrow.' Trending down!

Perhaps it is the great uncertainty and positive expectations of change that makes childhood so great. We know we are looked after, we know we are going to break away, we hope and expect to encounter romantic love - so much change ahead, and so many risks and yet this gross uncertainty provides the framework for mostly excited anticipation. Once we are settled and established the excitement of risk and extraordinary reward finds a new lesser level. Those of us, fortunate to have children, may to some extent feel the excitement anew through the lives of the children. And those even more fortunate throughout life keep their childhood sense of amazement and wonder before the many little delights on offer to the vigilant on an every day basis. Living means seeing, hearing, touching, smelling, feeling, and experiencing.

As children and youngsters we often are under a lot of pressure to acquire skills and learn even in the family environment. But failure doesn't mean we are out. It may mean more support, seeking new avenues, but rarely are threats used to make us perform. I strongly believe that even the working environment would gain by a stronger emphasis on support, showing people 'we will find a way together to achieve mutual benefit' rather than the harsher 'if you don't perform, you are out.'

For there to be a good relationship, it must be based on trust and confidence and support and not be eroded by daily expressions of doubt and suspicion. The approach we take tends to be self-fulfilling. Key for some kind of contribution is the attitude, the will to contribute. If the will is there, sufficient skills and personal growth can usually be attained that a meaningful contribution can be made. If an attitude of wanting to deliver cannot be brought out, then a separation of paths may indeed be the best way forward. It is no disgrace to make a change.

And a few comments on the choice lines from second Timothy.

There is a fine balance between humility and forthrightness and the optimum can only be established through experience. As long as there is enthusiasm and love, and purity of intent, there is every reason to step forward and dance. Lack of confidence is a bigger problem than overconfidence. Initiative drives the world. In the process we must try not to dominate to the extent that other opinions and good ideas get suppressed. And Bertrand Russell reminds us that 'Excess virtue is a vice.' 'For God did not give us a spirit of timidity, but the spirit of power, of love and of self-discipline.'

'If anyone competes as an athlete, he does not receive the victor's crown unless he competes according to the rules'. We may ostensibly perform better if we cheat, but it renders the whole game meaningless, and when found out we will be barred from further participation. Cheating means misunderstanding the premise of the activity, the game! The achievement isn't what it looks like if the game isn't fair. Neither the individual nor the general public can benefit by feeding on or being served lies.

'The hardworking farmer should be the first to receive a share of the crops.' A key part of Henry Ford's success was his desire to have the product priced so that those making it could afford to buy it. This was both fair and wise since it created a much enlarged market. Likewise the IKEA (furniture shop) success story is about availing quality product and design in such a way that ordinary workers can afford it. There is something revolting and inhumane in having people work all day and not be able to acquire even the bare necessities of life, i.e. food and shelter, in order that others overseas be able to buy cheaper goods and have ever increasing surpluses for luxury consumption. But is this really a concern for business? Decency and good morals are concerns for all. If not upheld, the lack of these qualities will cause resentment and hatred eroding good will and jeopardizing the success of any venture. Here we should note that low salaries are not evil as such. It becomes evil when there is no relation behind a full day's earnings and what is needed to buy the necessities of life. The most meaningful contribution we can make to the 'third world' is to try to help people help themselves by giving them a chance to earn enough for sustenance and that may well be less than accepted minimum salary in 'the industrialized world.'

When we meet foolish and stupid arguments we mustn't fall in the trap of descending to too low a level of debate. Key is to keep our cool and gently and politely try to lift the discussion. In this process nothing is gained by intimidation or embarrassment but the asking of a few humble questions may put things in perspective. Coming up with wrongful or accusing arguments don't mean that the person so doing is no good. It may well be pressure or other extraordinary circumstances that caused the digression or outburst. 'And rather than quarrel, be kind to everyone and not resentful.' Sooner or later honesty, moderation and genuine caring will bear fruit.

17. Titus

The blameless must be not overbearing, not quick-tempered, not given to drunkenness, not violent, and not pursuing dishonest gain. Rather he must be hospitable, one who loves what is good, and who is self-controlled, upright, holy and disciplined. *1: 7-8*

Encourage others by sound doctrine and refute those who oppose it; for there are many rebellious people, mere talkers and deceivers, and that for the sake of dishonest gain. *1: 9 - 11*

To the pure, all things are pure, but to those that are corrupted and do not believe nothing is pure. *1: 15*

In everything, set them an example by doing what is good. In your teaching show integrity, seriousness and soundness of speech that cannot be condemned, so that those who oppose you may be ashamed because they have nothing bad to say about us. *2: 7 - 8*

Slander no one, be peaceable and considerate and show true humility towards all men. *3: 2*

Doing what is good is excellent and profitable for everyone. But avoid foolish controversies and genealogies and arguments and quarrels about the law, because these are unprofitable and useless. *3: 8-9*

Warn a divisive person once, and then warn him a second time. After that, have nothing to do with him. *3: 10*

Our people must learn to devote themselves to doing what is good, in order that they may provide for daily necessities and not live unproductive lives. *3: 14*

Grace be with you all. *3:15*

Associations...

17 Titus

Surely we must make a profit - that is what our business is all about. We have all heard it and perhaps reacted "this is obvious" or "this is wrong." The dispute cannot be settled without looking a bit closer at what profit really is, i.e. how it is rightly defined. If you have profit mean benefit for mankind I would not hesitate to agree that any endeavor that has no benefit for anybody has little merit. If we define profit in a narrow accounting sense, i.e. a positive number after all registered cost has been subtracted form all registered revenue, then I would disagree that we can be sure that profit is an indicator of doing something positive and sustainable.

Quite often the incentive systems we find in large corporations are very narrow minded, encouraging participants to do little else but to pile the money up as high as possible. It is easy to see that this may well lead to the wrong kind of behavior in terms of taking short cuts and depleting resource and people in a way that erodes future earnings as well as other qualitative measures. Nowadays so much of what we are doing is not recorded by the traditional accounting.

Large corporations by definition have a great number of staff, often in the tens of thousands and many times exceeding one hundred thousand. These entities exist either as large government corporations, particularly in China and India but also in other countries or as national or multinational corporations with a strong exposure to the market and competitive forces. In both cases the majority of staff tends to be more or less alienated from the top echelon, who run the organizations, supposedly in the interest of the people or the shareholders, but more often than not for their own personal benefit. The powerful exploiting the weak! Does anyone think this will produce the ultimate commitment and team spirit through the ranks? I will leave you to provide your own answer. Particularly as rank and file get more and more capable and educated, the need for a greater sense of unity and Cause and *raison d'etre* becomes more obvious.

But isn't it impossible to reconcile the interest of the many mediocre with that of the few supreme? No, it isn't. How arrogant of us to regard the mediocre and average by disdain. Where have we acquired such limited and hostile view of humanity? Is it perhaps our school system? In fact not only the average, but – as John Ruskin asserts - even the last person in the world has a gift which, if brought to the fore and properly nourished, has the potential to render him or her of great benefit to humankind. This latter word says it all - humankind. One syllable without the other reduces both to factors lacking in soul, humility and love - the motor engines of any successful venture.

Profit needs to be put into perspective. True profit means seeking a way to operate which is sustainable and in harmony with the need to preserve nature and give respect, meaning and liberty to an ever increasing portion of mankind. Being imbued with this line of thinking and ensuring that your accounting and vision encompasses the inclusion of great and admirable goals for the disadvantaged inside and outside your organization, that is inspiring, that is something I and others are willing to give my time, my love and my life for. That is *Cause,* that is *Soul,* and that is *Spirit,* which has the potential to lend a divine motive to what you do.

That venture which does beautiful things to people with no discrimination as to race, color or gender or differences in intelligence or education and tries to develop all to something better more refined, allowing general participation in life and its fruits, that organization is on a viable and great trajectory. People will think: I want to work for it, I want to support it with my custom, and I want to invest in it. We are all emotionally driven creatures, and we are willing to go to great lengths for what we believe in. This approach does not mean that we should pay no attention to efficiency, price and other more conventional measures. All it means is that the soft goals and the hard goals must harmonize.

Most people would have some kind of understanding for this line of reasoning so in fact I believe it is not a completely new turn. All it requires is resetting our priorities a bit to be purposeful and motivational, admirable and human along with other more basic and technical goals. And when you are looking for a manager or chief executive, make sure these traits are there, or you may well be inviting disaster or decay or have many of your finest people leave, severely reducing your potential.

Accountants in their current role of accounting should be in the back seat recording what happens. Never let them into the front seat, never make it your prime goal that your accounting stacks up and have everything else fall in line. This is the opposite of vision. Vision can never be derived from adding or subtracting numbers. It has to come from within, be human and uplifting, and it has to touch people's soul to be effective.

18. Philemon

Paul's plea for Onesimus

Although I could be bold and order you to do what you ought to
do, yet I appeal to you on the basis of love. *1: 8-9*

If he has done you any wrong or owes you anything, charge it to
me. *1: 18*

Associations...

18 Philemon

There is not much point in ordering people around before you have
gained their confidence, and even then, if time permits, try to manage by
invitation rather than directive. Please and thank you serve as lubricants
to getting things done. Exercising rights isn't what leadership is about.
It is about maximizing every opportunity by bringing each and every
person to a point where they out of conviction and shared spirit want
to pull the very hardest they are able. Using formal authority, often lead
to less of a result, than when working through the spirit.

'If he has done you any wrong or owes you anything, charge it
to me.' This is one of the lines in the bible that made the strongest
impression on me as evidence of true friendship and love. Perhaps this
is the absolute core of Christianity and what Jesus is conveying when
he makes the ultimate sacrifice.

If - rather than pointing out how others transgress or disappoint or
err, from our safe corner of comfort - we just shoulder the negativity,

absorb it as our own, the world surely will be a better place. Many are those who are willing to take credit for anything positive or of merit that may have happened. How much more magnanimous is the opposite. If we react thus to things that have gone astray: 'it may have been my oversight, I will bring it right' regardless of the underlying facts, this is greatness leading to loyalty, faith and team spirit.

19. Hebrews

We must pay more careful attention to what we have heard, so that we do not drift away. *2: 1*

He is able to deal gently with those who are ignorant and are going astray, since he himself is subject to weakness. *5: 2*

And let us consider how we may spur one another on towards love and good deeds. Let us not give up meeting together, as some are in the habit of doing, but let us encourage one another - and all the more as you see the Day approaching. *10: 24 - 25*

We all have human fathers who disciplined us and we respected them for it. No discipline seems pleasant at the time, but painful. Later on, however, it produces a harvest of righteousness and peace for those who have been trained by it. *12: 9- 11*

Remember those in prison as if you were their fellow-prisoners, and those who are ill treated as if you yourself were suffering. *13: 3*

Obey your leaders so that their work may be a joy, not a burden, for that would be of no advantage to you. *13: 17*

Associations...

19 Hebrews

Visiting Kamakura last weekend and commanding a vast view of the mighty Ocean from an elevated point in one of the many Shrines there, it reminded me how inspiring and exciting the sea is. How it has created dreams of adventure and a better future for people through the millennia. And how it connects all things, places and people! The sea covers nearly seventy percent of the earth's surface. The first living creatures were of the sea about 450 million years ago. There is an old Chinese saying that the Sea is the greatest thing on earth because it is the lowest - whoever wants to be great must humble himself. Whether a little creek or a mighty river, both must ultimately bow to and pay homage to the all absorbing sea, which surrounds us all.

Looking out over the seemingly endless blue Pacific, I also think of our Baltic Sea summer island, beautiful beyond description, and how it lies at the other end of the very sea I am looking at. Rowing or swimming would in theory take me there if I had the stamina. And of course our lovely home in Auckland from which the same ocean is visible through the Palm trees. In spite of its size and might the Sea is not infinite or beyond the need for care and appreciation. In this book Jonah reminds of the sea and the birth of Christianity through Paul's travels, which would not have happened as it did without the sea. Water gives life and the sea is integral to all forms of living species, being not only a key source of food but as importantly, having throughout history served to connect people, enabling exchange of goods and ideas.

As with most things of great utility, the sea must also be respected for its might and ability to cause distress. Life and longing versus death and fear - different sides of the same coin, all represented by the same thing - in this case the mighty sea. Giving life and taking life! In his book 'Either/ Or, A Fragment of Life,' Kierkegaard says: "Let us be silent and listen to the music of the storm, its sturdy course, its bold challenge, the defiant roaring of the ocean, and the anguished sighing of the forest, the despairing creaking of the trees. It is true men say that the divine voice is not the rushing wind but the gentle breeze, but our ears are not made to pick up the gentle breezes, only to gulp in the din of the elements. And why does it not break through in still greater violence, making an end of life and the world and this brief speech, which at least has the supreme advantage that it is soon ended! Let it move and whirl away this naked cliff on which we stand, as easily as fluff before the breath of our nostrils. Take pity once more upon the world, open yourself again to gather everything in and protect us all safely in your womb." So what does all this mean? Beautiful and enigmatic like life itself.

The very word 'Hebrews' immediately brings to mind the conflict in and around Israel where things seem to be going from bad to worse in early 2002; forever escalating violence and no end in sight. The solution must be initiated by Israel and the USA who are the advantaged in the conflict. Israel needs to pull out of occupied territory and the borders must be guaranteed by international treaty and policing. This is the hottest political area in the world today and the most urgent for mankind to get a resolution to, as it stands in the way of universal love and brotherhood and puts about two billion of the world's people against each other. If such a great number of people are affected it means that all are affected.

In commenting on the few lines above, out of Hebrews, the word 'attention,' in the first excerpt, stands out. It holds the key to a better order of things. If we think a little bit less about how things ought to be and consider how they actually are, we have a much better chance to make real progress. Every organization I have come across is screaming out for better communication where perhaps the key issue is listening, i.e. paying attention to the constituent parts and people making up the organization. When directives and edicts are issued from somewhere remote and far away, often ignoring local conditions and restraints, no wonder there may be lack of enthusiasm in the execution. Whereas if we walk around and ask people - is this the best way forward? Please give any input you see useful to achieve the kind of improvement we are seeking to be the best we can be - this, if done well and sincerely, will bring a level of commitment otherwise unattainable. Such proper communication - involving showing respect, listening, care, and attention - will require time. But this is not to be seen as a cost but as an investment. No harvest without sowing.

Weather you are religious or not, of this or that religion, your morals and ethics will be noted and seen and if you break the commonly held rules for decency and forthrightness it will come back and haunt you. Why? Because you are on a win- lose philosophy and all the people you cause to lose for you to achieve success are sure to get back at you, if in no other way by despising you and making your winnings bitter and less enjoyable.

Whenever we have to try to address underperformance or undesirable behavior we should put ourselves in the culprit's shoes and remember that we also have shortcomings and can do better. We should try to sit on the same side of the table rather than on opposite. This is where we are; let's try to find the best way forward for you. A concern for the individual, rather than just endless requirements that others adjust to fit the mold, works wonders. Even if the person doesn't fit in any longer, that may just as well be a sign of health as a shortcoming. If we always try to build and support people to get the most out of life, surely we have the foundation for loyalty and team spirit.

There is a risk with modern technique that we don't need to meet in person to the extent we used to. This is not progress. It is the end of life. Meeting up with other people to discuss, learn, encourage and progress - that is life. We must beware that we don't become so efficient that all that renders life worth living is done away with. As globalization progresses we find people working together all over the world. But if people don't meet up in person at least once a year you cannot really talk of a team.

As with everything it is a matter of finding the right balance. Frequent meetings benefit from being short and focused. If it is the once a year gathering it benefits from being informal, looking to increase friendship and understanding - creating good soil for nurturing future ideas and co-operation - rather than solving specific issues. If we feel elated when communicating with remotely located colleagues it is good for teamwork and results. This only happens if we meet from time to time to establish and renew personal friendships.

20. James

Everyone should be quick to listen, slow to speak and slow to become angry, for man's anger does not bring about the righteous life that God desires. *1: 19 - 20*

Do not merely listen to the word and so deceive yourselves. Do what it says. *1: 22*

Mercy triumphs over judgment. *2: 13*

Faith by itself, if not accompanied by action, is dead. *2: 17*

Ships, although large and driven by strong winds, are steered by a very small rudder wherever the pilot wants to go. Likewise the tongue is a small part of the body, but it makes great boasts. Consider what a great forest is set afire by a small spark. *3: 4- 5*

Associations...

20 James

This week we saw the ending of the Salt Lake City Olympic winter games. Although quite spectacular in many ways, there is inevitably something staid over the whole concept. In some ways it has become perhaps too competitive and distant from what is normal and healthy. Why do we have to pitch nation against nation? Why do so many of the participants find it necessary to take performance-enhancing drugs? And does the taking of such drugs really matter? And for all the activities that require the judgment of judges, how do we avoid that such judges vote their affiliation rather than the quality of the performance? Is there too much money involved? Perhaps part of the games could be randomly combined teams from several nations. In Ice hockey for example would it not be even more entertaining to see teams combined by lot from the pool of available Olympic players where each team has a minimum of four nationalities represented? Would this not serve better the goal of bringing people together and creating bridges between peoples and nations? These are many unanswered questions, but something seems to be needed to spark it all up with a few surprises to have the games make more sense in the third millennium.

My week was dominated by a conference in Hong Kong on how to take our business forward. As usual there was just a little bit too much of regression, shrinkage and centralization in the brew and all the loyal lieutenants - the survivors - convincing each other that it makes a lot of sense. I just have a feeling that on these occasions intangible value isn't given due respect, mainly because it isn't well understood. But is it really going to be successful to have no better idea than cost cutting and forever making things leaner and more specialized? Many individuals know that shrinking reduces opportunity and that the trend line suggests that all will be redundant in due course. Further centralization makes less room for human traits and the whole human being becomes less whole and more of a cog. This may well make it harder to retain and attract new talent.

I had an opportunity to contribute to some balance by giving a talk to the conference on 'Diversity' with twenty slides and a recorded piece of music to go with every slide. What a difference a day makes - and the difference is you; People who need people are the luckiest people in the world - we are children needing other children; together we stand - divided we fall; just hum a merry tune - just do your best and take the rest, and sing yourself a song; everybody deserves to be in the *limelight* sometimes; always look on the bright side of life; the best of times is now - live and love as hard as you know how; life is just a bowl of cherries – the sweet things in life, to you were just loaned, so how can you lose what you never owned?; lift us up where we belong; you'd better start swimming or you'll sink like a stone; you can be better than you are, you can be swinging on a star; you may say I'm a dreamer - but I'm not the only one.

The key messages were putting things in perspective and making sure there is room for enjoyment and love. We have everything to gain by making women well represented in all forums and finally and most importantly, everybody, all, each and every one, regardless of gender, race or religious affiliation has a beautiful core somewhere, giving him or her great potential for growth and improvement. Any talent review or personnel policy that doesn't endeavor to bring out the talent in **all,** carries a serious opportunity cost. Both the music and the messages were well received in the group of senior managers, half of whom were female.

The letter to James underscores the need for perseverance, listening and acting on convictions. How relevant these three qualities are in today's world! If we combine these with love and mercy there isn't much more we need in terms of clothing to be well dressed for every occasion in life. True faith is in the acting, in the everyday practicing of that which you hold high and believe in - the rest is just adornments which often are unnecessary and may reduce the natural beauty. Practicing beats preaching. Nothing leads like example.

21. First Peter

G race and peace be yours in abundance. *1: 2*
You know that it was not with perishable things such as silver or gold that you were redeemed from the empty life handed down to you from your forefathers. *1:18*

Love one another deeply from the heart. *1: 22*

Rid yourselves of all malice and all deceit, hypocrisy, envy, and slander of every kind. *2: 1*

Wives, your beauty should not come from outward adornment, such as braided hair and the wearing of gold jewelry and fine cloths. Instead it should be that of your inner self, the unfading beauty of a gentle and quiet spirit, which is of great worth in God's sight. *3: 3 - 4*

Above all, love each other deeply, because love covers over a multitude of sins. Offer hospitality to one another without grumbling. Each one should use whatever gift he has received to serve others, faithfully administering God's grace in its various forms. *4: 8 - 10*

Be self-controlled and alert. *5: 8*

Associations

21 First Peter

After a week away from my 'Associations' due to many overseas visitors, I sit down again on a Sunday morning and wonder if I have anything to put on paper. Having learned and accepted that even the plainest of days is a miracle in terms of its wonders and offerings, and that on the eve of our lives we would give almost anything to have a new quite ordinary day of health and trivial experience, I spurred myself on to make an attempt.

As I write the term visitors, a line from 'The Letter's of the Younger Pliny' came to mind. In response to a dinner invitation he writes: "I will come to dinner, but only on the condition that it is simple and informal, rich only in Socratic conversation, though this too must be kept within bounds; for there will be early morning callers to think of." Even when we let loose and enjoy ourselves, it is healthy to keep the concepts of care, generosity and love at the back of our mind, and keep the merriment within such bounds that it doesn't impair the beauty and many opportunities of the next morning and day.

For me this means talking about a few interesting things to put life in perspective, trying to sing and laugh and dance, enjoying good food and drink, and accepting that gaiety and social intercourse is the healthy way of life and not something we should allocate only a small portion of our time to. But it all has to have some moderation such that productive thought and work and contemplation of things beautiful aren't lost in the process. No wine after midnight and no sleep after eight o'clock in the morning are rules I like to impose on myself.

The last week has reminded us that interacting with visitors and friends is very healthy and enjoyable. If we are too singular, either by ourselves, or inside a family, it is easy to get a bit exhausted with oneself and/or each other, and socializing widely is a very healthy expansion and diversion. When Aristotle says that man is a political animal I think he means that man is a social animal. Interacting with others is a sort of acupuncture for the soul - any tension within your system or among your core small group of people eases and goes away when you get into thinking of others and it helps to make us count our blessings and realize that the trivia that worried us isn't even worth considering. 'Oh what I would have given then to have no greater problems than I face today' says holocaust scarred Victor Frankl in his book 'Man's Search For Meaning.'

As we have set up eight new homes in the last sixteen years we have frequently experienced moving away from our friends. Perhaps the most important step for finding a new place agreeable is to as quickly as possible build a network of friends. They are everywhere; it is just a matter of making the effort and finding them. And of course once you have a good friend, you should never let go again - amigos para siempre! It may not always work out like that, but it is a reasonable proposition to nurture and cherish friendships as the most valuable of currencies. With our houseguests I think we have particularly enjoyed gathering around in the cooking of meals and the sharing of a good bottle of wine. At a dinner party at home a few weeks ago my wife told me: "I am grateful God gave you some academic talent because you are pretty hopeless in the kitchen." So having houseguests often has the benefit of making the preparing of meals a more social and collaborative process.

Rereading the lines from First Peter above I am again touched by how they are not only beautiful but eternally relevant, each and every one of them. What better wish can there be for friend and foe than hoping that Grace and Peace may adorn their lives? It is the beauty on the inside that matters and to seek improvement of spirit and soul is a finer undertaking than amassing money or things. Love is the ultimate remedy for the ills of mankind. If its practice and promulgation don't get you the results hoped for, at least you know you have pursued and promoted the only true way. We must try to use our gifts to lighten the hearts of others. These are universal indisputable truths that must color all we say and do.

22. Second Peter

M ake every effort to add to your faith goodness; and to goodness, knowledge; and to knowledge, self-control; and to self-control, perseverance; and to perseverance, godliness; and to godliness, brotherly kindness; and to brotherly kindness, love. *1: 5-7*

If you possess these qualities in increasing measure, they will keep you from being ineffective and unproductive. If anyone does not have them he is shortsighted and blind. *1: 8-9*

A man is a slave of whatever has mastered him. *2: 19*

Make every effort to be found spotless, blameless and at peace with him. *2: 14*

Be on your guard so that you may not be carried away by lawless men. *2: 17*

Associations...

22 Second Peter

How do we stay on a high and be happy, grateful and confident at all times?

We cannot.

No one can do it all the time. If everybody were happy all the time the concept would loose its very meaning. We mustn't despair that we cannot be as radiant and contented and happy as this or that person. This or that person also has his or her up- and downswings. Swinging without motion is unexciting and meaningless.

This morning I woke up before six because I had promised to drive my son to his friends as they were all going to Tokyo Disneyland for the day. I find that when I have made some kind of commitment like that I always wake up one or two hours before by some internal body signal. Two little things were weighing me down this morning. One was that my wife who left for Singapore and New Zealand a few days earlier had asked me to make a few music CD's with Italian music for a planned get-together with friends in Auckland and I couldn't get it right. Now I will have to call her and ask for precise instructions again, which is a bit annoying and embarrassing. Then last night we got information in the mail-box that across the road from us a new building project will be started and continue for one full year which will take away our park like view and replace it with a three story building. Great!

How can one be happy about that?

One cannot.

But does it really matter? Today I will have plenty of time to read and write and to go for a run in the sunshine. Tokyo is a temporary abode for us with plenty of opportunity to see and learn and travel locally and regionally. I feel a strong sense of appreciation at work, at home and among our many friends from near and afar. Our home is very nicely laid out with things we like and have accumulated from many countries. Our cleaning lady was here yesterday so all is spotless and I had the privilege to sleep in new, clean and ironed sheets. In the near future I have a vacation trip planned to New Zealand and Singapore and a bit further out one to Spoleto in Umbria, where Linda has booked us into a most exquisite little hotel for ten days, and then on to Sweden.

In Italy I will try to get to Assisi to acquaint myself further with the famous Francis of Assisi (Francesco di Pietro di Bernardone, dead 1226). I have three beautiful sons that are a credit to their parents and an abundance of good friends whom I love. I am listening to Jussi Björling singing my favorite song: O Sole Mio. I am well into reading Anna Karenina, which may not be more than a novel of love, but I love it anyway, unashamedly. "I don't accept life without love - no help for it, that's how I am made." A daily dose of Leo Tolstoy is enriching my soul. I have yet to find anything he has written which isn't beautiful.

So why should I worry about such trivialities as those described above?

I shouldn't.

And I won't. It is human, I believe, to get irritated when things don't go your way. It is divine to be alive and have access to so much beauty and opportunity. And I guess I believe that we can and should all try to train our minds and reasoning to increase our levels of experience and happiness. The Grand Pa clock next to me gives nine strokes indicating that the day is still young and holds plenty of experiences and opportunity in store.

Paul's second letter to Peter reminds us of the importance of goodness, knowledge, self-control, perseverance, kindness and love. If we think about these things and put them high up in our consciousness it helps us deal with small or big setbacks and put them in perspective and thus we are better equipped to be a credit to others and to ourselves. The best that can happen to us in any one day is to cause someone to smile and experience affection and warmth of heart. The chance for this happening is naturally so much higher if we manage to stay cheerful, happy and merry.

We all know that no one is perfect, but to live is to have faith, and to have faith is to be in pursuit of improvement, in pursuit of happiness, in pursuit of wisdom and in pursuit of perfection. The pleasure lies not in discovering the truth, but in searching for it. As the goal is as elusive as the rainbow's end, we must never allow the wrong means to be used in our pursuit of the end. The end moves away as we approach it so key is to enjoy the road and appreciate how it is adorned with beauty and flowers.

Don't be a slave of anything other than tolerance and love. What were those problems again? I cannot remember. This is when I go for a run in the sunshine.

23. First John

If we walk in the light, as he is in the light we have fellowship with one another. *1: 7*

Whoever loves his brother lives in the light, and there is nothing in him to make him stumble. *1:10*

Whoever hates his brother is in the darkness; he does not know where he is going, because the darkness has blinded him. *1: 11*

Let us not love with words or tongue but with actions and in truth. *3: 18*

Let us love one another, for love comes from God. *4: 7*

God is love. *4: 8*

Whoever lives in love lives in God, and God in him. *4: 16*

There is no fear in love, but perfect love drives out fear, because fear has to do with punishment. The one who fears is not made perfect in love. *4: 18*

Associations...

23 First John

If you believe in living in love, if you believe in pursuing all inclusive good, to the limit of your ability, for your fellow man, without any discrimination, that's it. That is the essence of religion. When asked if I am religious I say yes and no. I am not religious in the conventional way, but I feel religious in being in awe and admiration for the intrinsic good in most human beings and all the wonders of creation and nature. By no means do I understand how it all came together and I don't think any one else does either. But the beauty of the soul, expressing itself in love and generosity, and the many wonderful things we see around us, I consider indisputable and divine. Living in the spirit of love and compassion surely is the meaning of religion. This is not something we do on Sundays, Easter or Christmas. This is not exclusive for any one of many world religions. This is something done all around the world, all days, twenty-four hours a day. It requires neither church nor temple.

Faith to me is faith in the beauty of human nature and its strong natural desire for love and compassion. Having faith that these aspects are strong enough to make the world a better palace to live in and that the ultimate quality of life comes by promoting universal love! John Ruskin, the 19th century English writer suggests: "Richest is he who has had the greatest helpful influence on others." Although I strongly believe this makes a lot of sense, it is more a manifestation of love than of logic.

Relocating to Tokyo after twenty-two months in Singapore, it feels like a bit too soon given the time it takes to build up friendships with staff, customers and others. However, friendships can always be maintained, regardless of a little distance, and the prospect of new additional friends is exciting. I remember an investment advice from Switzerland to always sell early. When everything is going well and relationships are thriving, that is the time to make the move. The only way to establish the point of a peak is on the way down. Then it is too late. Being on the up is what renders life meaningful.

We all know that we will never get there, wherever we are heading. Getting to the goal is not the objective - the objective is the way and the journey of continuous improvement, starting with improvement of self. Goals tend to be static whereas life is dynamic. But what about all the hassle of packing up, and setting up again? Bertrand Russell, the distinguished author and philosopher, reminds us that a necessary ingredient in happiness is effort. Periodic challenges and achievements are building blocks for a full life and must therefore be welcomed. When we look back on life, these changes are the things that provide richness and wealth of experience. And it is the things that we don't do that we regret, not the things we do. No moss can grow on rolling stones.

24. Second John

I ask that we love one another. And this is love: that we walk in obedience to his commands. *1: 5*

I have much to write to you but I do not want to use paper and ink. Instead I hope to visit you and talk with you face to face, so that our joy may be complete *1: 12*

Associations...

24 Second John

After some time away including a train holiday from Rome to Stockholm via Milan, Vienna, Prague and Berlin, a few weeks summer holiday in Sweden, three weeks of wind-down and saying fare well in Singapore and six weeks of getting established in Japan, I am back to my associations again. Separately I have written a few notes about my train trip and my first impressions and experiences in Japan.

One of the most interesting and perhaps useful messages of the bible is to meet adversity and hostility with love. This is perhaps a bit counter intuitive and a challenge that requires commitment and training of the mind. But since adversity often is caused by humans, the way to try to reduce such adversity in future is to always put rage and anger aside and replace it with love. It may not be natural, but it does make a lot of sense. A quality future is more important than achieving a tit-for-tat equality relating to past events. I had my wallet stolen in Rome and I was given some phony money in exchange for one hundred US dollars in Prague and in addition I experienced a few other little irritations. If we try to build a better society where more feel as if they are participating and are treated well in spite of digressions, we can hope to reduce the reasons for people to act selfishly and anti socially.

As much as we will never get rid of expressions of evil and bad behavior, if we can reduce it we are doing something right. I heard president Clinton comment in relation to China's Human rights record and their membership in the World Trade Organization when he said "I believe more in the open hand than the clenched fist." More often than not this has to be the way - trying to argue, convince and showing the way by role-modeling, rather by condemnation and persecution. Education, communication and involvement serve the same purpose. Rarely does the clenched fist achieve lasting improvement.

So I tried to manage my emotions related to these events and not let them influence my immediate or longer-term world outlook. Most things like these are quite trivial, and material loss can quite easily be replaced. Getting angry or downtrodden just adds to the pain and set back. On top of some small misfortunes, you are punishing yourself. Someone said, 'There are two things we don't need to worry about - what we can influence and what we cannot influence. As for the former, we just make an action plan and get on with it, and as for the latter we are well advised just to disregard it.' Many things are not objectively this or that but are in a certain way because of our perception of them. If we learn to manage that perception the issue may not in fact exist anymore.

Love is to forgive and forget; to give someone who doesn't deserve it a second chance, to turn the other cheek. If you allow love to invade and imbue body and soul and test all your actions and reactions to ensure full alignment with Love, you are already home. This is religion at its finest.

We are essentially the sum of all the impressions we make on others. If we don't communicate or make any impression on others, we gradually fade away. A kind thought, a friendly smile to someone we meet, showing some compassion to man or any living creature helps define us and make us real. A brief email to someone is nice, a phone call is great, a letter is even better, but best is to make the effort to be there and communicate with all your senses, the feeling of unity and oneness with others. Nothing communicates sincerity better than real time face-to-face sincere two-way interaction. Being with someone is to demonstrate that you find it worth your while to spend time together. Just as sending a check may help, true conversion and demonstration of heart and interest requires that you be there physically in support of people for the creation of joy and for consolation and easing of pain.

25. Third John

I pray that you may enjoy good health and that all may go well with you. *1: 2*

I have no greater joy than to hear my children are walking in the truth. *1: 4*

Do not imitate what is evil but what is good. Anyone who does what is good is from God. *1: 11*

Associations...

25 Third John

Today I sit down to write my 66th note of 'Associations,' which means that I am about to complete the second stage of my project. Why the 25th book is addressed last when there are two more books of the New Testament is simply because I didn't write them in straight order. Order is good but a bit of disorder can make things more human and alive. Unpredictable and irregular may offer greater experiences than too much systematization. Compare the twenty-four hours a day vibrancy and pulse of chaotic New York City to the slow-moving, predictable and neatly laid out D.C.

The second and third letters to John are the shortest books of the bible being half a page each. The shortness of the letter makes me think of the brevity of life. Seneca wrote a book titled 'The Brevity of Life' and the two lines from that book which stuck in my mind are: "He who has little is not poor but rather he who wants more." Although I read this book in Swedish this line came out well in English. The other one line is: "I shall consider myself owning nothing, other than what I have given away with dignity." Rather than storing up wealth, it is more rewarding to store up credit with our friends and loved ones - a credit that is there for us if we need consolation or support ourselves. To be fair and objective we need a little bit of both wealth and love. But the Bank of love has no accounting and no auditor and is not required to make a profit, so, unlike tangible enterprises, it cannot fail.

When I first met the prominent author Catherine Lim (I subsequently read and enjoyed many of her books and cherish our ongoing friendship) at a function in Singapore and we talked about reading and literature she asked me right away three hard questions, one of which was: 'What do you think happens after death'? I said I don't know, which is perhaps the first thing that came to mind, but of course, I wanted to qualify that. Somehow I feel that some of these eternal questions need reconsideration and perhaps rephrasing. So many queries set you up to answer either black or white whereas perhaps a lovely tune of music would be a better response. Or grabbing the nearest bunch of flowers and say - look at these beautiful flowers. Will they wither away? Yes. Will there be new flowers to adorn tomorrow and the day after, this year, next year and a thousand years from now? Yes. So does life for flowers end or stop? I have three fine boys. Will there be a next generation of children? Will they have children? Is there an end to life?   Beauty and wisdom are eternal.

Cicero said that as for what happens after death there can be only two alternatives. "Either there is nothing more, and then we have nothing to worry about, or there is heaven for the souls in which case the coming of death is greatly to be desired. Either lacking unhappiness or being positively happy, there cannot be anything to fear." The one thing we know remain after death is the credit gained by good and right actions. And Socrates suggests that as all things are generated out of their opposites, life comes from death just as death comes of life.

In The City of God St Augustine says: "No longer do we begin to live in this dying body, than we begin to move ceaselessly toward death. Man begins to die as soon a he begins to live." This undisputed fact in combination with Psalms 90:12 'teach us to ponder how few our days are that we may live each one wisely' should prompt us to live well, merrily, happily and lovingly. And as the saying goes; we shall be held accountable for all the permissible pleasures we haven't enjoyed. Primo Levi, with first hand experience of Hitler's death camps, says that death places a limit on every joy, but also on every grief.

I am currently reading Anna Karenina and loving it. Although the book is of a great number of pages, will I get to the end? Of course I will! Does that worry me? No.

My experience of life teaches me there are an infinite number of fine moments to be encountered and enjoyed? New opportunities to experience beauty in the form of performing and expressive arts and in fine deeds and meeting great people are constantly on offer. It was my reading last night that brought me on to this subject. Levin's brother (in the aforementioned book by Leo Tolstoy) is dying and he doesn't want to bring his young wife Kitty to the scene to spare her any agony. To his annoyance, she insists on coming along and proves to be infinitely more competent in communicating warmly and personally with the dying brother than Levin himself, who is just lost for proper action and conduct.

This very thing happened with my wife Linda and me in relation to my father's death. I loved him very much but didn't quite know what to do. She did and it was beautiful and, as I perceived it, very well received. Don't try to be correct - be close, be loving and hearty, relieve and ease any pain, clean and comfort, touch and support, don't think - just act naturally and caringly. This is the kind of sortie to pray for. Both St Augustine and Shakespeare say that worrying about death can only take beauty out of life. The coward dies a death every day in his worries but the valiant dies but once. Nurture and cherish what you do have, don't let what you don't have bother you or take the appreciation and beauty out of life.

Our parents and their parents before them spent the better part of their lives trying to set their children up with a good start for a better life. If, towards the end of our personal journey, we know that we have done our best, even in the smallest of ways, to make the world a better place, this I believe is a tremendous consolation. If we have only narrow-mindedly and egoistically extracted short-term personal pleasures, perhaps at other people's expense, we may be reproaching ourselves.

Most of us have received so much from loving parents and many others during our formative years and later, that we have to give as much and a little more again back, if we can, to those we are able to reach and support, influence and love. Any investment should rightly have some return. The purpose of all our acts is to achieve something perceived as good. This is how world human capital can and have grown over time. And how about those who have got a raw deal and not been exposed to motherly or parental love? Even for these people the best way forward is to try to give that which they may never have received and to have good hopes for a late harvest. Even for the starving the hope lies in the continuous successful sowing. And in compassionate sharing!

When Jesus talks about eternal life, to what extent is it metaphorical? How does it work? No one quite knows. It falls under the categories of the metaphysical and faith. Thus I have to recognize that I cannot add too much here. Like with so much in life we must decide for ourselves what we believe and what makes sense. Proven and demonstrated certainty just isn't available to many essential mysteries of life.

Just as it is difficult to prove this or that belief, it is equally difficult to disprove, suggesting humility and tolerance around these questions. But I do think that the benefit of eternal life can be experienced already whilst living this life, like a feeling, a tangent and a trajectory lending quality to the earthly years we do know about. If we are convinced about the merit of beauty, compassion and love this can provide a joy and elation, which gives the deepest appreciation for the gift of life and renders death almost insignificant. Beauty, compassion and love remains. What is permanent and eternal is merit, having made an effort of lifting the species a little bit higher.

On his death-bed, according to Ammianus Marcellinus, Emperor Julian said: "My friends, nature is requiring of me that which she has lent me; I return it to her with the gladness of a debtor who is clearing himself. I receive death as a favor. I have cheerfully faced peril. I have always loved peace." (From Anatole France's 'Of Life and Letters')

This the 21st day of March in the year of 2002 and all the cherry trees are overflowing with millions of pretty flowers in a cascade of fragile, fleeting beauty. People tell me that it is a bit early. No one can remain untouched by it. First the flowers, then the leaves then the fruits, then the harvest, then the losing of the leaves and then again the blooming of the flowers! And this cycle for as long a period back as man can remember; highly symbolic and most delicate.

From the short book second John we can be encouraged by the following: "I pray that you may enjoy good health and that all may go well with you. I have no greater joy than to hear my children are walking in the truth. Try to do what is good."

26. Jude

The Sin and Doom of Godless Men; a Call to Persevere

Certain men whose condemnation was written about long ago have secretly slipped in among you. *1: 4*

They are clouds without rain, blown along by the wind; autumn trees without fruit and uprooted twice dead. *1: 12*

These men are grumblers and faultfinders; they follow their own evil desires; they boast about themselves and flatter others for their own advantage. *1: 16*

These are the men who divide you, who follow mere natural instincts and do not have the Spirit. *1: 19*

Associations...

26 Jude

God is good and Jesus is Love. These are fundamental Christian beliefs. Commit yourself to benevolence and love and you are away. Buddhism is very similar as is the core of most other religions. All religion is seeking o promote that which is good. Religion only become bad when used to purposes for which it was not intended. In fact wisdom - good sense and judgment, the thoughtful application of learning - is impossible without a framework of benevolence and affection. And breaches against humanity always involve some kind of narrow-minded self-seeking, without proper regard for others.

In all areas of life you find clever people who seem to be good citizens, but at the end of the day are doing nothing but trying to preserve and enrich themselves at the expense of others. True religion is about leaving that attitude behind and making sure that all we do align with the common good. Disregarding others will always pose a threat to your comfort and life style and is often connected with falsehood, secrecy, dishonesty and exploitation. Choose this path and you will never be able to rest from possible repercussions in the form of hate and avenge.

Such negative approach and life outlook, which, like a positive outlook, is self-fulfilling, may well have its roots in lack of self-experienced love, compassion and security. Therefore the easiest and most obvious remedy is for as many as possible to act out empathy and generosity, particularly when it looks ill deserved, because that is when there is a chance to make a turn in someone's life. To love your friends and good people is easy. To try to enlighten digressers is more of a challenge. Each of us must try to show the way by our actions and behavior.

In mathematics, if a statement is not valid or correct in one case of a hundred, it is false. In human interaction and in social sciences, things tend to be true and valid if they are correct most of the time, or true in general. A good compassionate, caring society may not drive out all ills, but it will work on most and a repressive, harsh and punitive society no doubt leads to a lower quality life. The successful iterative search for a more balanced and harmonious state of affairs requires that more people are imbued with compassion and the broader interest of all humans, 'absolutely everybody.'

In the corporate world, as well as in government and society at large, we must become more discerning in promoting the right kind of leaders. Character needs a much higher weighting than hitherto. Achievement amounts to nothing, if it is not for a good purpose or aligned to what is in the public interest and sustainable life and environment. This is not idealistic - it is highly realistic - and acting in what is ultimately self-interest. If your activity nurtures bad will, suffering and hate you may short term look like making progress, particularly as per current accounting practices. But the amount of intangible liability build up may just be waiting to show its real face and ruin your business or position. We need to be clearer about values, and profit is not a value - it is the outcome of doing things well.

What about the pressure from shareholders, and the need for growth and increased returns? The point is that share holders are better served in the long run by people who avoid moral short cuts and who don't look the other way when values are breached, but commit to ethics and Love. This last word would seem to be out of place in any discussion of business, but most would agree that it is core to what we are about and what we hold dear in life. If what we call business doesn't align with what we think is the nucleus and meaning of life, then we are seriously out of line and need to rethink our ways.

This is the morning of Sunday the 30th September. The big black crows are screaming outside. I have been for an hour's reflective walk with the dog - and brought home some fresh bread from our wonderful bakery. Last Friday I went to a seminar on 'Executive Compensation' and 'Economic Value Added.' Both these concepts are being driven by accountants who are specializing in making things measurable. However, we mustn't compromise our important goals for goals that are easier to measure. The measure of what we want to do has to be secondary and subsequent to our goals, not the other way around. To assume that competent sensible adults - leaders who deserve to be leaders - are mainly driven by bonus formulae is manipulative and tending to not give values, often crucial for survival, their proper weighting. We need to think again.

A common business practice originating in America is the use of disclaimers. These disclaimers have been driven by the fact that the high number of (often self-serving) lawyers, particularly in the US, have created very litigious societies. We need to turn 'negative' disclaimers, into positive 'claimers.' Lets state on our faxes, emails and letterheads what we are about - the values against which we test all our activity. If we visibly hold up the purpose of our activity before the eyes of our customers and staff and the public we can hope to improve on leadership and the ongoing implementation of values. Getting it right in relation to customers, staff and the public is in fact a prerequisite to successful shareholding and thus the first is primary and shareholder wealth is the secondary flow on effect of getting the formula right.

27. Revelation

I know your deeds, your hard work and your perseverance. *2: 2*
I have placed an open door before you that no one can shut. *3: 8*

You say, 'I am rich; I have acquired great wealth and do not need a thing.' But do you not realize that you are wretched, pitiful, poor, blind and naked? *3: 17*

They were told not to harm the grass of the earth or any plant or tree. *9:4*

Give back to her as she has given; pay her back double for what she has done. Mix her a double portion from her own cup. *18: 6*

It shone with the glory of God, and its brilliance was like that that of a very precious jewel, like a Jasper - clear as crystal. *21: 11*

On each side of the river stood the tree of life, bearing twelve crops of fruit, yielding its fruit every month. *22: 2*

Whoever is thirsty, let him come; and whoever wishes, let him take the free gift of the water of life. *22: 17*

Associations...

27 Revelations

Reading this last book of the Bible again, I reflect that there are some harsh and grim passages there, prescribing torture and grief. However, I set out to find what is inspiring and uplifting in the Bible and not to take every passage literally. One of the sayings from Confucius is to absorb from learning what makes sense and leave the rest by the wayside. Thus my quotes above do not necessarily give a true reflection of the almost vindictive nature of Revelations, but rather highlights that conduct which is consistent with the core messages of benevolence and love. To me the book is not holy - it is the message of love that is sacred. Many acts and events as recorded in the bible are incompatible with love, forgiveness and compassion.

When you are fortunate to have many friends - connected through love - you don't need to fear anything. The support and unity takes away your vulnerability. Whoever might be dependent of you will be supported and carried by your friendships, should anything happen to you. And since you are connected with many people, if one plant fades away, the others remain to absorb the rays of the sun and the water of life. People come and go; the legacy of love lives.

Walking the streets of my Tokyo suburb, Yoyogi Uehara, I am amazed at how small the streets are, how pedestrian everything is, how every house on certain streets are owner occupied small businesses, making the environment very vibrant and alive - people walking, talking laughing, chatting moving about everywhere. More often than not I see it in the dark as when I return from work it is already late. And particularly in the dark, with all the little lamps lit and all the shadows playing up by all the people moving about, it makes me think of Hades. I have had the same feeling in India a few times. A sort of charming mystique that lies on the border between life and death in the sense that it feels so eternal! There is nothing much to remind you of the passage of time. In this small-scale environment (in the middle of the thirty million people city) everyone you meet and talk to seem loving and keen to help and every shop visit yields a sense of friendship. This is my positive vision of the land of death - plenty of people calmly and lovingly working together and not a lot of space.

Setting up our home in Tokyo is testing of perseverance - and yet we are lucky with plenty of support and not too constrained by lack of money. Almost everything is in Japanese, all manuals, all answering machines, all instructions, everything. A nice new phone system combining fax and phone with plenty of buttons to press and many functions no doubt, but out of reach because of lack of instruction. A new computer bought from a Japanese salesperson that didn't speak English. Unpacking it yesterday it had some instructions taped across the screen - usually saying something like - Warning, you have to do things in this order or it won-t work - totally unavailable instructions as they are in Japanese characters, which we don't understand. And we couldn't get it to work so will have to try to get a technician here next week - in itself a challenge - as service is something computer sales people around the world regard as a necessary evil to be minimized.

We got our car last week with a brilliant navigation system. There is an English version where a lovely female voice tells you where to turn and how to drive to get anywhere in the country. But, you guessed it; all instructions are in Japanese. We have now preset our six most important addresses - work - hospital - school - home - club - airport - but to set anything new requires an interactive twenty step process which just isn't possible without knowledge in Japanese. The answer - learn Japanese, let the expert set any new important destination, drive by ordinary map, take the train - so it's not the end of the world - it just requires good humor and perseverance.

The door that no one can shut has to be about opportunity, learning and love. You and I are our own masters in this respect and with a strong enough commitment, outside influence cannot turn our faces away from the light. What a gift of God to be presented with a long string of days (not endless though as we are reminded in Psalms 90:12) each and everyone offering plenty of opportunity for learning and love.

Wealthy is he/she who has many friends and lives a considered, loving life. We must get business, politics and economics to fit into this formula or we will exhaust both human and natural resource. Money and efficiency at the expense of love and care is not a very good trade off. We need to continually demonstrate to others and ourselves that our work is in line with the humble serving of mankind - if not, we must think again. We must not deplete the beauty and resource of the world - any action, good or bad defines us and determines the climate in which we live. As for the fundamental commitment to love and compassion this line says it all: 'Just like a tree standing by the water, I shall not be moved.'

Bibliography

A People's Tragedy, the History of the Russian Revolution   Orlando Figes

A Short Life of Swami Vivekananda   Swami Tejasananda

Anna Karenina   Leo Tolstoy

As A Man Thinketh   James Allen

Bodies in Rest and Motion   Thomas Lynch

Childhood, Boyhood and Youth   Leo Tolstoy

City of God   St Augustine

Contemplation   Franz Kafka

Earthbound Travels in the Far East   Tiziano Terazani

Either or, A Fragment of Life   Soren Kierkegaard

Encyclopedia Britannica

From Third World to First   Lee Kuan Yew

Ignatius Loyola

Man's Search For Meaning   Victor Frankl

Mencius   tr by David Hinton

Mere Christianity   C S Lewis

No Ordinary Time   Doris Kerns Goodwin

Notes From The Underground   Fiodor Dostoevsky

On Agriculture   Cato and Varro

On Life and Letters   Anatole France

Paul, In The Mind of an Apostle   A.N.Wilson

Romance of the Three Kingdoms   Luo Guan Zhong

Rights of Man   Thomas Pain

Unto This Last   John Ruskin

Sand, Wind and Stars   Antoine de Saint Exupery

Simple Truths	Fulton Sheen
Stalin's Nose	Rory McLean
The Analects	Confucius
The Brevity of Life	Seneca
The Conquest of Happiness	Bertrand Russell
The Consolation of Philosophy	Ancius Boethius
The Ecology of Commerce	Paul Hawken
The Kingdom of God is Within You	Leo Tolstoy
The Koran	
The Letters of the Younger Pliny	tr by Betty Radice
The Politics of Hope	Jonathan Sachs
The Prince	Macchiavelli
The Wealth and Poverty of Nations	A.N.Wilson
Trust	Francis Fukuyama
Utopia	Sir Thomas More
War and Peace	Leo Tolstoy
What Men Live By	Leo Tolstoy

And primarily, HOLY BIBLE – NEW INTERNATIONAL
VERSION
Published by Hodder and Stoughton